The Artful Ribbon

BEAUTIES IN BLOOM

The Artful Ribbon

BEAUTIES IN BLOOM

Candace Kling

C&T PUBLISHING

©1996 Candace Kling

Editors: Liz Aneloski and Barb Konzak Kuhn

Copy Editor: Judith M. Moretz

Technical Editor: Sally Lanzarotti

Cover Design (ribbonwork and photography):
Candace Kling and John Bagley

Cover Design (mechanical): Jill Berry

Book Design: Jill Berry

Illustrations: Rik Olson

Ribbonwork Design Assistant: Zenaida Cosca

Photography: John Bagley

Published by C&T Publishing, P.O. Box 1456, Lafayette,
California 94549

ISBN: 1-57120-020-7

Library of Congress Cataloging-in-Publication Data

Kling, Candace.
    The artful ribbon: beauties in bloom / Candace Kling
        p.   cm.
    Includes index.
    ISBN 1-57120-020-7 (alk. paper)
    1. Ribbon. 2. Ribbon flowers. I. Title
TT850.5K56 1996
746'.0476--dc20   96-18923

Fray Check is a trademark of Sewing Notions Division of
  Risdon Corporation
NO FRAY is a product of Brohman Distributing Company
Carb Othello is a registered trademark of Schwan-Stabilo
Coats Dual Duty Plus is a registered trademark of
  Coats & Clark, Inc.

Printed in Hong Kong

10 9 8 7 6 5 4 3 2 1

*Photo previous page spread: Wedding gown embellished with ribbon roses
for Constance Rowena Power-Heinse, 1995.*

Contents

Dedication

To those milliners,

seamstresses, and dressmakers

who were paid for their time,

but not for their inspiration.

Vintage flower sprays.
c. 1920s. Collection of
Sandy Fisher.

*M*any share my passion for ribbonwork.

Generous collectors kindly lent their beautiful ribbon treasures to photograph for this book. Although we can't all own the vintage works pictured here, the photos are my attempt to share these wonderful collections and my love of ribbonwork with you. For a brief moment I was able to possess each of the vintage works pictured in this book. I marveled at their materials, tenderly touching their shiny or sparkling, silken surfaces.

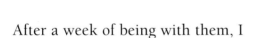

After a week of being with them, I began to dream about exquisite ribbon flower bouquets, made of shimmering silks with metallic threads and ruffled edges, in a vast array of luminous colors. These works were new to me, but the ribbons used were the most fabulous vintage ones I'd ever seen. I realized then how deeply I was affected by this wealth of flower fantasies. My hope is that you will be affected by them also and that they will inspire you to want to make your own ribbon flower bouquets.

Double-faced ribbons, popular in the 1920s, were especially effective in creating more complex shading in everything from dimensional rosebuds to bow loops. Collection of Arlene Baker.

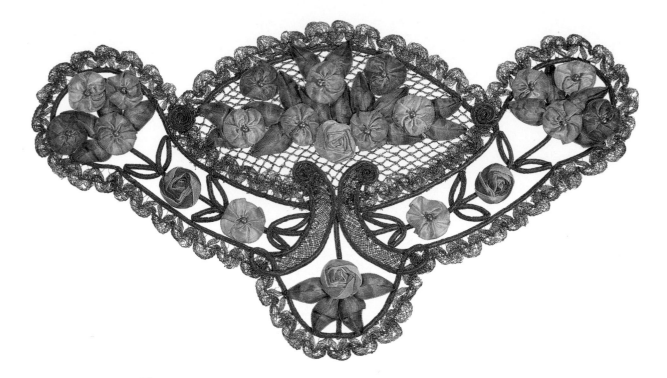

I've heard it so many times, "I've always loved ribbon." It's like music to my ears. Ribbon is a thread back to childhood, to a time of fancy party dresses, multicolored hair ribbons, and presents made spectacular with big satin bows. Many remember a family member (mother, aunt, or grandmother) who created this work. Others recall doing it themselves earlier this century. Sometimes the memory is fond; sometimes it's tinged with regret—that the knowledge has slipped away and the treasures are long gone. The lucky ones have saved and cherished their ribbons, buttons, bits of lace, sachets, and lingerie bags, christening gowns and baby bonnets. For those without a family, they've made one up by haunting garage sales, flea markets, and antique shows, collecting their "heirlooms" and bringing them for me to see.

Sometimes I only hear about a special treasure. It arouses my imagination nonetheless. Who could forget a student's description of "an ivory dress with blue and pink roses, and a sash that wrapped around the waist like a piece of music"? The work itself seems to elicit a romantic response.

I am struck by the fact that the museum collections I have explored over the past fifteen years don't contain the bulk of the vintage flowerwork I have seen. That work has been brought to my classes from private collections. I can only surmise that when it comes time to distribute the family estate, some heirlooms will be sold or offered to museums while others are kept. Much of the ribbonwork is small and intimate. It can be framed or made into sachets or pillows. Vintage hats can adorn our "boudoirs." The ribbonwork pieces, found tucked away, find their new homes within the family. There is always someone who wants and will appreciate a cluster of velvet pansies or a spray of silk-petaled rosebuds. They are simply too beautiful to resist. There is a universal love of flowers that cuts across the ages. They are never out of style.

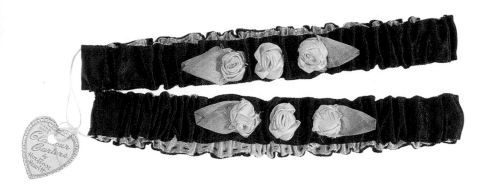

But learning to sew has gone out of style, and some of the knowledge that women of past times carried with them has been lost to us today. Society no longer expects its young women to be proficient in stitching in order to be marriageable.

The fact that we lack their training might be discouraging to you when you first see one of the many vintage texts on ribbonwork that have been reproduced in the last ten years. Not only is the language different, so are the materials. For several centuries now, fashion has dictated that ribbons change yearly. Each season the colors change, the patterns change, and the textures change.

Different manipulations of the ribbon and variations in the stitching were in vogue at different times. Instruction varied from country to country and book to book, and most often it was brief.

Because the beginnings of stitching were often taught hands-on, not through books, there are gaps in the oral tradition. Part of my research mission has been to unearth and then to translate into current language what information I have found. Sometimes, where parts are missing or when only the finished flower remains, it has been necessary to intuit their process, or to invent some "new" way to teach it.

For this text, I've tried to develop a fuller and more consistent instructional language both in illustrations and in words, giving the techniques easy nicknames where possible. The "Invitation to Use this Book," which follows, will get you started easily, answering your most basic questions. But don't skip the technical sections; they're filled with tips and tricks.

Ribbonwork can be (and was) a combination of manipulated ribbon, fabric and lace, silk ribbon embroidery, standard embroidery, beads, cords, and tassels. Women in other eras weren't specialists. They were mistresses of many needle arts and they mixed them.

With the explosion of women's magazines at the end of the nineteenth century, the world was teeming with information in this area. Whole magazines, books, and booklets were devoted to ribbonwork. There was so much information that a shorthand developed. Women were so knowledgeable they didn't need detailed instructions. A drawing of a single petal might be all you would get as explanation for a whole corsage. It was expected you already knew what size to stitch, how to finish off, and how to compose.

Women knew how to stitch and they knew how to sew; straight stitching and plain sewing, as well as decorative flights of fancy. They also studied drawing and painting. It was part of a gentlewoman's education to learn these things. Trained in flower painting and china painting, they were grounded in an awareness of the structure of flowers. They observed nature and were exposed to botanical drawings. Even the

Opposite page: Striking for its bold color, this vintage spray is secured to heavy wire rather than to crinoline. Its overlapping petals are a variation on the "puffy leaf," but with just one selvedge hand-gathered to form a pleated central spine. c. first quarter of the 20th century. Collection of Meron Reinger.

Left: Set of vintage wands; one a mirror, the other a powder puff, c. 1920s, fit perfectly the category of "boudoir fantasies." It has been suggested that these were a gift befitting a mistress. Collection of Catherine Manzini of Ages Ahead.

most modest booklet on the making of crepe paper flowers, from Dennisons Manufacturing Company in 1922, recommends that in order to understand the flower you are going to make, you should take apart a real one and examine it. Women in other eras wrote poems and made cards containing images of and references to flowers. Each flower had its message that you were expected to know. Even the colors had individual meanings. Much of this knowledge is lost to us today, although we still appreciate the sentiment behind a gift of deep red roses.

In the past, without modern refrigeration and transportation, many months went by without the sight of fresh flowers in the house. We take for granted and cannot imagine how exotic and expensive it was to have flowers out of season. To fill this void, women surrounded themselves with objects adorned with blooms of all kinds, carved, painted, and stitched in a myriad of forms. Ribbonwork afforded them the luxury of flowers in winter.

Fortunately, flowers remain eternally popular. They never lose their allure. Men and women throughout the centuries have all had a love of flowers. There have been times throughout history, though, when this popularity reached a zenith. The first quarter of the twentieth century was one of these times. The wealth of vintage beauties pictured in this book from the 'teens and 1920s reflects this popularity. What a pleasure to hear a student reminisce about being taken to San Francisco in the 1920s to The City of Paris department store, notions department, to choose ribbon flowers for her party dress.

To meet the enormous demand at the time, women worked in *ateliers*, the workrooms of France, producing ribbon flowers on crinoline for export. For many women over the centuries needle arts were not a hobby. They counted on them for their livelihood. They were professionals. The vintage texts reflect this when they proclaim that the quickness and cleverness of a certain bow will "help you turn a tidy profit."

Whether you plan to make or just to look, whether it's for profit or for pleasure, I think you will find ribbonwork lends itself beautifully to the interpretation of nature and flowers, with its rich palette of colors and lush tapestry of textures. There is a surprising simplicity to many of the techniques and endless pleasure in watching the ribbon come alive to your touch.

Left: Crinoline held these imported buds in place. c. 1920s. Collection of Jules and Kaethe Kliot of Lacis.

Opposite page: Vintage fan purse decorated with clustered "baby rosettes." c. 1915. Collection of the Oakland Museum of California, History Department.

An Invitation to Use this Book

Ribbonwork is fun and easy.
You might want to dive right in, but know these few things
before you start.

What is RW?

RW is your ribbon width. All the ribbon formulas in this book are measured in ribbon widths (RW). For example, 5 RW is the width of your ribbon times 5. One formula works for any width of ribbon. You never have to convert using math. This single formula will work no matter what width ribbon you choose.

To measure your ribbon, first establish your ribbon width on a surface with pins or marks. To do this, place your ribbon down vertically on your work surface. Put a pin (or mark) alongside each selvedge edge of ribbon as shown. This is your Ribbon Width (RW).

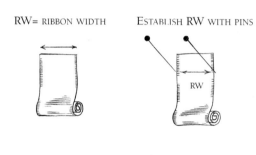

RW= RIBBON WIDTH   ESTABLISH RW WITH PINS

Now turn your ribbon horizontally and move it along the pins or marks, counting out your formula in ribbon widths along the selvedge edge.

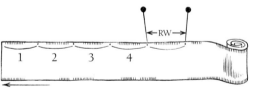

COUNT OUT RIBBON WIDTH

Introducing Crinoline

Crinoline is a lightweight buckram that looks like starched cheesecloth. It is important enough to the success of ribbonwork to have its own chapter in this book. As you will see, single flowers, buds, and leaves, as well as whole flower sprays, are created on crinoline. In a pinch, you might use lightweight interfacing or netting.

Playing with Wire-Edged Ribbon

Wire-edged ribbon has tiny wires woven into its selvedges during the manufacturing process. It is readily available in fabric, craft, and floral supply stores. It's also fun to play with. You can gather, stitch, form, and shape it. It is available in polyester and rayon-acetate. Try both—experiment. The wire helps you coax your ribbon into a myriad of flower forms. The "Textured Finishes" chapter will help you explore the possibilities. Wire-edged ribbon has its own set of eccentricities. These are discussed in "Getting Technical" chapter.

The look of the finished flower or leaf is achieved because of the wire edge. Sometimes the wire is the only thing holding the manipulated ribbon in place. No glue or stitching is possible.

Variegated and Ombre Defined

These terms refer to the change in color that occurs across some ribbons, from selvedge to selvedge. For example, ribbon is ombre if the color blends from purple to lavender. Ribbon is variegated if it changes color, say from purple to green. You can make two different-looking flowers from the same ribbon by reversing the color at the edge.

Tools and Supplies

A basic sewing kit with a couple of additions will get you on your way:

- ❋ Scissors-two types (to cut ribbon and to cut wired ribbon)
- ❋ Milliners needles (longer with long eyes)
- ❋ Heavy thread
- ❋ Ball head pins
- ❋ Crinoline (¼ yard)
- ❋ Chalk marker (Carb Othello pencil®)
- ❋ Tape measure
- ❋ Duck clips (page 108)
- ❋ Fray Check™ or NO FRAY
- ❋ Padded work surface

See "Getting Technical" and "Crinoline" chapters for a detailed discussion of these tools and supplies.

Let's Go Shopping

Three yards each of several flower colors and two yards each of several leaf colors is a good start. The colors should be complementary. Buy a mix of variegated/ombre and solids, wired and unwired. Remember, the wider the ribbon, the more you'll need. And not all ribbon is woven—some types are made of paper. Paper ribbon is not as sensitive or as flexible as woven ribbon. The more commonly used ribbons for flowerwork are ⅝", 1", and 1½" wide. As you become more involved, buy your ribbons by the roll. It's cheaper.

Explore your local fabric, craft, and floral outlets. You'll find a source list on pages 138 and 140 with a list of numerous suppliers of ribbons, crinoline, flower stamens, and more (wholesale, retail, and mail order).

Stitching Secrets

When making ribbon flowers, start with your most comfortable stitch length, the one that seems to come naturally. You'll relax in the work if you can pull this off because it's more automatic. Still, it's important to have a repertoire. Some effects cannot be created without ⅛", ¼", or ½" long stitches.

As you work, you'll find these rules may apply: The wider the ribbon, the bigger the stitch. The thicker the ribbon, the bigger the stitch. For example, if you're using velvet, you might start with ¼" long stitches.

To decide on a stitch length, dive in! Try one (petal, leaf, etc.) and if it doesn't work, change your stitch length and do another. In the time it takes you to puzzle over which stitch length might be right, you could have made three and compared them.

Secure from the Start

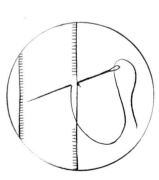

Secure your knot before you begin stitching. When beginning a row of stitches, knot your threaded needle. Pull the needle through the ribbon and backstitch around your knot. If your knot is on the selvedge, backstitch over the selvedge.

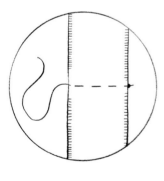

Tug the thread to test whether the knot is secure. A very open-weave ribbon may require backstitching a second time.

When drawing together petals, or a ruffle, into a circle "make your knots kiss." To do this, finish your last petal, then backstitch, and knot. Don't cut your thread. Direct your needle back through your beginning knot. Tug tight, closing the gap to make the knots kiss. Hold the ribbon together, backstitch, knot again, then cut the thread.

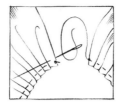

Finding Your Way

You might ask, "Why doesn't my flower look like the one in the picture?" The answer is, you didn't make the one in the picture. Ribbonwork is individual. Each maker puts her personal signature on the ribbon with her stitch size and her touch. It's almost impossible to copy exactly. Embrace this.

Some of the vintage samples in this book were made with silk ribbons that are no longer available. Use the photos for inspiration. There's a bounty of beautiful ribbons available to us today. Each of these has its own unique characteristics which will affect your creation. Look to "The Dance" chapter for some thoughts on putting it all together. Experiment and have fun.

Vintage postcard.
Collection of
Meron Reinger.

STARTING SIMPLE

These first flowers are almost childlike in their simplicity. They are based on variations of a simple ruffle. You'll need only a minimum amount of sewing knowledge to make them. Just because they're so easy doesn't mean you will discard them as you learn the more complicated ribbon flowers. These beauties become the chorus in your ribbon flower bouquet. Make them by the dozens and tuck them into your more elaborate compositions.

If you're going to dive right in without reading "An Invitation to Use this Book" (page 14) there is still one thing you need to know; RW (Ribbon Width). All the formulas in this book are given in relation to the width of the ribbon (RW). No math, no measuring just count off ribbon widths on the edge on your ribbon and cut. See "Getting Technical" chapter—What is RW? (Ribbon Width) on page 103.

Double Ruffled Rosette

Cut a 5 RW length of ribbon. Stitch the raw edges together (French seam if possible) to form a tube, with the seam to the outside. Make a running stitch around the tube, slightly above the halfway mark.

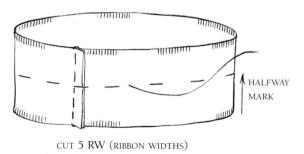

HALFWAY
MARK

CUT 5 RW (RIBBON WIDTHS)

Opposite page: Detail of "baby rosettes" on vintage fan purse on page 13. c. 1915. Collection of Oakland Museum of California, History Department.

Pull in the thread and knot to form the gathered center. Flatten into a two-layered flower.

Tack the flower to crinoline. See "Crinoline" chapter (page 116). Stitch down the outer edge with beads if desired. Add stamens or a center. See "Berry Buds, Stamens & Centers" chapter (page 64).

Rosette with Ruffled Center

Cut and stitch into a tube as for Double Ruffled Rosette, but this time with the seam to the inside. Make your running stitch a third of the way down from the top edge.

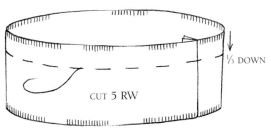

"Double ruffled rosettes" are secured with seed beads to this vintage purse. Collection of Jennifer Osner.

Finish as in Double Ruffled Rosette. The raw seam shows slightly in the center ruffle.

Basic Rosette Figure 8

This double ruffle is simple enough to be the first ribbon flower you teach a six-year-old!

Measure out a 7 RW length on your ribbon; mark both edges or crimp them with your fingers. Fold at this point, doubling the ribbon length to 14 RW. Then cut. Starting from the midpoint of your ribbon, secure your knot by backstitching over the selvedge. Stitch as close to the selvedge as possible, ending at the cut edge. Different stitch lengths produce different effects. See "Stitch Lengths" (page 109).

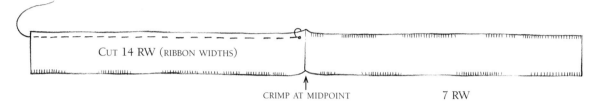

CUT 14 RW (RIBBON WIDTHS)

CRIMP AT MIDPOINT   7 RW

Draw in your gathers to about ½". You may have to "walk along" the gathers with your fingertips several times to condense them this much. (Don't be afraid to tug tightly if you've used heavy thread and your knot is secured.) Backstitch and knot. Spread to form a circle.

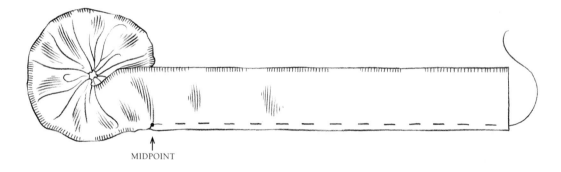

MIDPOINT

Repeat this process on the other side of the ribbon, again starting from the midpoint. Once completed, the two raw edges should meet at the center back. Tack to crinoline and add beaded, budded, or buttoned centers, plus a few leaves for accent. See "Green" chapter (page 76). Use a variegated/ombre ribbon and your rosettes will be two different colors.

Rosette Figure 8~ Two Ribbons Together

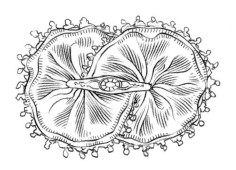

Cut two 16 RW lengths of ribbon (wired only). Use different colors, or reverse the colors on a variegated ribbon. Stitch as in Basic Rosette Figure 8. Treat the two ribbons as one. This gives your rosettes a double ruffled edge. Don't let the two ribbons remain sandwiched together. Lift and shape the "upper skirt" to reveal the "petticoat."

Rosette Figure 8~Ruffled

Cut a 20 RW length of ribbon. The extra ribbon will make your circles more ruffled. Fold in half and crimp at the midpoint.

Stitch as in Basic Rosette Figure 8.

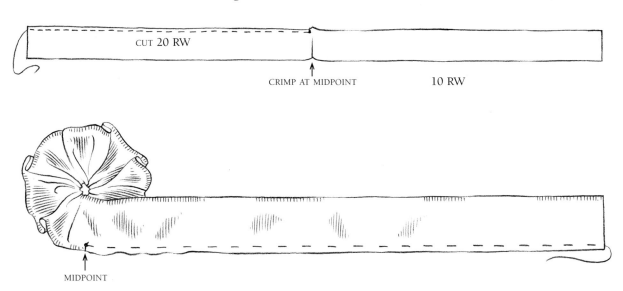

CUT 20 RW

CRIMP AT MIDPOINT   10 RW

MIDPOINT

Lace with a decorative ribbon or set off with flower centers.

Rosette Figure 8~
Outer Edges Gathered on Wire

Cut a 20 RW length of ribbon (wired only). Fold in half and crimp at the midpoint. Stitch as in Basic Rosette Figure 8.

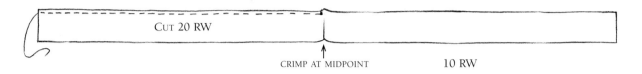

CUT 20 RW

CRIMP AT MIDPOINT   10 RW

When the stitching is complete, pull the wire to gather the ribbon at the outer edge of each circle.

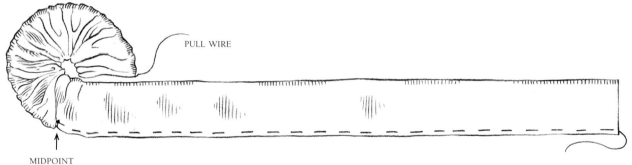

PULL WIRE

MIDPOINT

Trims with "baby rosettes." Courtesy of Elsie's Exquisites.

Your rosettes will be gathered inside and out.

Liven up your cuff buttons, dress up a bar pin at your throat, or decorate a barrette with this rosette. Although the goal is to create nice tight centers, you needn't be concerned with this if you are going to cover them anyway (with buttons, etc.).

Baby Rosettes

The baby rosette has been a staple in baby and lingerie work throughout this century. The beauty of this technique lies in its simplicity. You can execute it with ¼" (and smaller!) ribbon. Flowers made in this way are the "chorus in your ribbon flower opera." They are your filler flowers. Although they may not be as elaborate individually, a mass of them will add to the richness of your bouquet.

Basic Baby Rosette

Cut a 9 RW length of ribbon. Making a clean cut is important if you are working in miniature. If you cut off-grain, fray it out and cut again. Use Fray Check or NO FRAY if necessary. If your ribbon has wire, remove it from the inner edge (the edge that will be the center of your flower). Start stitching ⅛" in from the raw edge. Backstitch over the selvedge to secure. As you stitch to the other side of the ribbon, round the corners. "Hug the selvedge" as you continue stitching, rounding the second corner and stitching across to the other side to form a curve. Leave ⅛" at the raw edge as you finish stitching. The curves create two ¼" tails of ribbon you'll later be able to hold while you stitch your center.

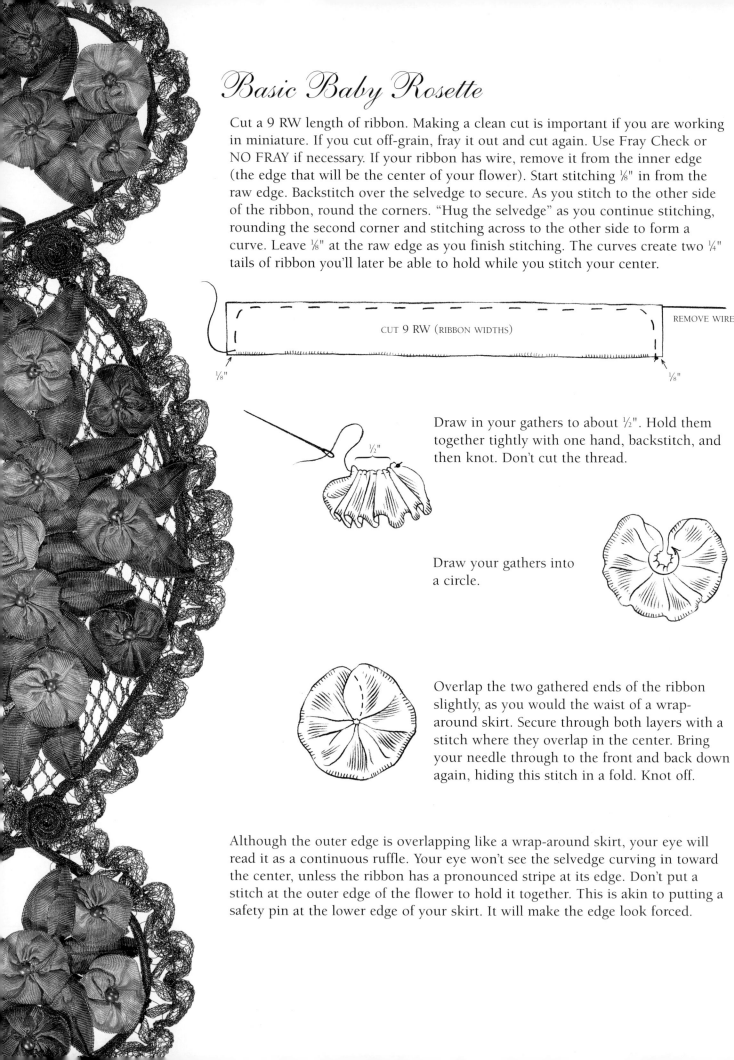

CUT 9 RW (RIBBON WIDTHS)

REMOVE WIRE

⅛"   ⅛"

Draw in your gathers to about ½". Hold them together tightly with one hand, backstitch, and then knot. Don't cut the thread.

½"

Draw your gathers into a circle.

Overlap the two gathered ends of the ribbon slightly, as you would the waist of a wrap-around skirt. Secure through both layers with a stitch where they overlap in the center. Bring your needle through to the front and back down again, hiding this stitch in a fold. Knot off.

Although the outer edge is overlapping like a wrap-around skirt, your eye will read it as a continuous ruffle. Your eye won't see the selvedge curving in toward the center, unless the ribbon has a pronounced stripe at its edge. Don't put a stitch at the outer edge of the flower to hold it together. This is akin to putting a safety pin at the lower edge of your skirt. It will make the edge look forced.

Baby Rosette ～ Ruffled

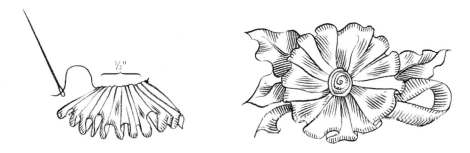

CUT 11-15 RW

REMOVE WIRE

Cut an 11-15 RW length of ribbon to make a flower with more ruffles. If the ribbon length is any longer, you may run into problems drawing the ribbon down into a small center. Using slightly larger stitches will help in achieving this. Stitch as in Basic Baby Rosette.

½"

Baby Rosette ～ Ribbon Folded in Half

Fold ribbon (wired only) in half lengthwise. Use this new width to measure 9 RW (or greater), then cut. Stitch as in Basic Baby Rosette. You will be stitching along the folded edge.

FOLD

CUT 9 RW

NEW RW
(WIDTH OF FOLDED RIBBON)

Separate the two layers to create the double ruffle of this rosette.

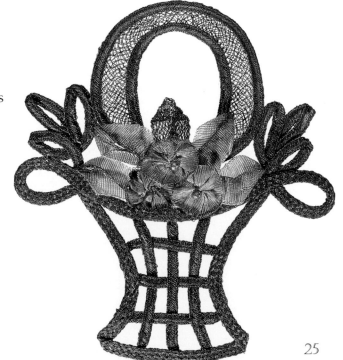

Opposite page: "Baby rosettes" with gold bead centers are coupled with metallic lace tape and net in this detail of a passementerie piece (page 8) from the first quarter of the 20th century. Collection of Bette Greer.

Below: "Baby rosettes" are the buds in a basket in this vintage composition. c. first quarter of the 20th century. Collection of Carole Sidlow of Romantic Notions.

Baby Rosette~Spiraled

Cut a 30 RW length or greater of ribbon. Stitch as shown.

CUT 30 RW OR GREATER

Draw in and spiral your ruffle around its center wrapping in a circular motion, tacking to crinoline to secure it. See "Crinoline" chapter (page 116). You can play with the degree of your gathers, loosening or tightening them, to create different effects. How much you overlap your rows of ruffles will also alter the finished look.

Baby Rosette~Two Ribbons

Put two ribbons together and stitch them as one. They could be the same or different widths, but definitely use two different colors. Use the RW of the wider ribbon to calculate the length of ribbon to cut. Stitch as in Basic Baby Rosette. Use a longer stitch because of the thickness of the two ribbons.

CUT 9 RW OR GREATER   REMOVE WIRES

"Baby rosette" trims.
Collection of
Zenaida Cosca.

Baby Rosette ~ Ribbon Folded Off-Center

Experiment with the position of the fold. The placement of the selvedges will change the look of the finished flower and allow you to customize its width. Stitch as in Basic Baby Rosette.

Baby Rosette ~ in Profile

Cut an 11 RW length or greater of ribbon. Stitch as in Basic Baby Rosette, but don't form into a circle.

CUT 11 RW OR GREATER   REMOVE WIRE

Tack to crinoline in an arc shape.

Cover the gathers with a calyx with stem. (See Index page 142.) Add stamens if desired.

Make a second slightly longer ruffle and layer the two onto crinoline to create a double ruffled flower (see photo).

Baby Rosette ~ Triple in Profile

CUT 9 RW OR GREATER   REMOVE WIRE

Make three separate rosettes.

Tack to crinoline as shown, with the center petal slightly covering the other two. Combine the three rosettes to form one.

Opposite page: Contemporary "baby rosettes in profile" rest on a bounty of 1920s ribbon. Collection of Meron Reinger.

Cover with a calyx with stem. (See Index page 142.)

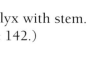

A ROSE IS A ROSE

Spectacular roses will bloom beneath your fingertips. This technique is the current favorite ribbon flower. It's popular for a reason: it's easy, versatile, and fast. You can also individualize it, adding your personal touch of color, texture, and placement. Most ribbons are easily coaxed into its form. Repeat this rose, always with a different result. It's as pleasing in miniature as in large scale.

Ruffled Roses

Cut a 36 RW length of ribbon; 1½ yards of 1½" wire-edged ribbon is easy to start with. You can also make this rose with unwired ribbon, but it will require more stitching. You have a decision to make with variegated and ombre ribbons: darker color to the inside, or outside? It would be natural to say dark to the inside. It seems logical, but there is a beauty to putting the light to the inside; it gives the flower an internal glow.

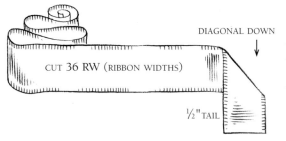

DIAGONAL DOWN

CUT 36 RW (RIBBON WIDTHS)

½" TAIL

Start with one end of the ribbon folded down diagonally toward you. The folded ribbon forms the edge of a square. Leave a ½" tail.

Fold this portion in half to "close the book," as shown.

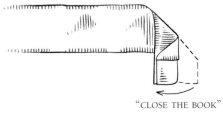

"CLOSE THE BOOK"

Opposite page: A cluster of cabochon buds forms the closure for this 1920s pink satin bed jacket. Collection of Jules and Kaethe Kliot of Lacis.

Put your thumb ⅛" away from the fold. Then fold again, against your thumb, to begin to roll.

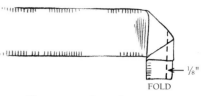

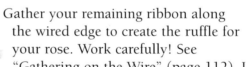

Roll up the tail. Continue to roll. Notice that the outer selvedge edge is beginning to form a circle. Roll around several times.

Make two ⅛" tucks, in the second and third rolls at the base of the bud. Wire-edged ribbon will do this easily. The tucks give your coiled center the appearance of opening. Try not to pinch or flatten the outer edge of your wire-edged ribbon, especially near its coiled center. Hold it gently. Protect it.

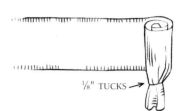

Below: Stamens with puffed centers for the "spent" rose. Collection of Candace Kling.

Opposite page: Contemporary roses grace a vintage ribbon lace jacket. c. 1960. Collection of Brigid Finucane.

Place this budded center on a piece of crinoline and secure with a pin from the back. Be sure to catch the selvedges of your bud with the pin. Your budded center will stand up in the air.

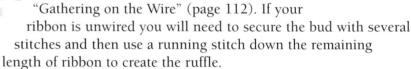

Gather your remaining ribbon along the wired edge to create the ruffle for your rose. Work carefully! See "Gathering on the Wire" (page 112). If your ribbon is unwired you will need to secure the bud with several stitches and then use a running stitch down the remaining length of ribbon to create the ruffle.

Pin the crinoline, with its bud and ruffle, to a padded surface to compose your rose in one of the six ways described on pages 34–35. If you've made this rose before, but didn't know about crinoline, you may have wrapped it very tightly, stitching all the rows of ruffles to each other near the center on the back. If you used ombre/variegated ribbon, the contrasting color is completely hidden by the multilayers of ruffle wrapped so tightly. You paid for the variation in color, but you aren't seeing it. With crinoline you can spread your ruffle because you'll stitch down into a backing. As you spread the ruffle you may see hints of the crinoline peeking through. If this is a real concern, put a piece of fabric on top of the crinoline before you pin down the coiled center. It could match the ribbon, or be an accent, a surprise color. If you use black crinoline it will disappear into the shadows. See "Crinoline" chapter (page 116).

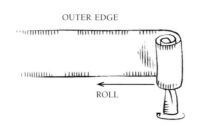

#1 ~ The Target

Flowers are not targets, but sometimes they do engage you in a direct gaze. Use this variation if you want the rose to look straight ahead. Spiral the ruffle around the bud, but not too tightly. When you come to the end of your ruffle, draw the raw edges together tightly in your fingertips and wrap with the pulled wire. Clip off the remaining wire. (Don't use your good scissors!) Tuck the end under to finish.

#2 ~ Budded Finish

Make a bud at the end of your ruffle. To do this, smooth the last 4"-5" at the end of your ribbon. In the same way you began your rose, diagonal down, close the book, and roll it up. This bud interrupts the smooth round finish of your flower. If you keep rolling backward, you'll have two equal-sized flowers.

#3 ~ Center Off-Center

Make the center of your rose off-center. Start by stacking the rows of ruffles underneath each other on one side of the bud and radiating them out on the other. You might add a bud at the end, as in #2. Flatten the coiled center to accentuate the gesture of a head turned slightly to the side.

#4~Center Off-Center, Zigzag Ruffle

After wrapping your ruffle several times around the center bud, make it wrap backward and forward on just one side. You could do this with continuous ribbon, or by adding another ribbon at this point. It could be another piece of the same ombre or variegated ribbon with the colors reversed. You might add a bud at the end as in #2.

#5~Internal Petals

Make several pleats in your ruffle as you wrap it around the center. (This is not necessarily two pleats in the fourth row as the illustration suggests.) Put as many pleats as you want, wherever you want. The pleats give you a sense of internal petals and break up the monotony of the spiral. Gathering on the wire makes a wavy ruffle. When stitching by hand, you can make a very ruffly ruffle. If you want your wired ribbon rose more ruffled, add pleats to it. You might add a bud at the end as in #2.

#6~Separate Petals

Add petals of a different color and/or material. See "Petals" chapter (page 44). Decorate them with ruffles, beads, or embroidery. The colors you choose are a part of your uniqueness, your signature on the ribbon.

You don't need to make a target. You might make your budded center off-center. This will affect your petal placement. You'll want to place your petals on only one side. When your flower is in three-quarter view, its head is turned slightly to the side. Place your petals on the side opposite the coiled center.

Rosebuds

Instead of making continuous ribbon flowers like the "Ruffled Roses" (page 31) you can make separate budded centers. Watch them grow as you add outer petals and ruffles, using the layering method described in "Crinoline" chapter (page 116). Mix different colors and textures. Sometimes rosebuds are stitched very flat, which can add contrast in your work to the very dimensional ruffles and petals that surround them. This also makes them a practical choice for embellishing clothes, pillows, and quilts.

You won't always need to cut your ribbon to begin. Sometimes you should play or experiment first and let the flower emerge in your hand. Do you wrap tightly or loosely? Do you want a densely petaled center to your bud, or a more loose and open look? The flowers will speak to you if you let them. Save the decision. Don't cut the ribbon too soon. Look and decide, then cut.

Basic Scalloped Rosebud

Using wire-edged ribbon, double twist it at approximately 2 RW intervals. (These intervals can be uneven.) Use your thumbs to form strong scallop shapes, one thumb on the front of your ribbon, and the other on the back, with nails facing one another. Try making ten as a start, but don't cut your ribbon, you can add more if you like. Diagonal down a ½" tail. Fold to "close the book" and begin to roll up, cupping the lozenge shapes around the bud. Keep it loose. When you have decided on the number of scallops, cut your ribbon. Tuck the end under to finish the bud.

Pin to crinoline from the back and tack to secure. Trim off excess crinoline. Add outer ruffles or petals if desired. See "Layering Crinoline" (page 120).

DOUBLE TWIST   DIAGONAL DOWN

½" TAIL

FOLD
"CLOSE THE BOOK"

Scalloped Rosebud ～ with Knots

Knot the ribbon every 2 RW. Use your first knot, with a short tail hanging down, for the center. Roll and wrap the remaining cup-shaped lozenges around your bud, but not too tightly. Finish as in Basic Scalloped Rosebud.

← ROLL

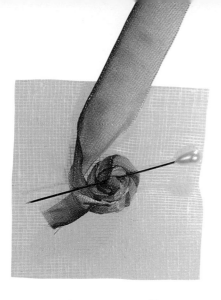 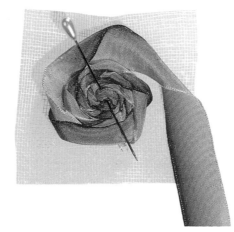 

Hatpin Rose

Named the "3 Minute Rose" in a text from 1923, this flower was not tacked down. It was secured to your hat with its decorative pin, just for the day, with a ribbon that matched your outfit. In this way, women "dressed" their hats.

This version, however, is stitched to crinoline and the pin is removed. Cut a 30 RW length of ribbon (wired or unwired). Fold ribbon in half lengthwise, at the tip. Pin it to the center of the crinoline using a florist's pin or hatpin and leaving a ½" tail. Catch 1/32" of the ribbon and attach it to the crinoline with your pin.

This becomes the center of your bud. You want it to be small and tight in contrast to the larger, more airy outer petals. First, roll and twist the beginning of the ribbon tightly, like a rope. Then lay it under the pin as you wrap it around and around the center. Start to loosen the rope twists as you do this. Spiral the ribbon in a twisting motion outward and away from the center. As the bud grows the selvedges will begin to tuck under the previous row as you wrap, and the outside edge will take on a faceted look. Tuck the end under and pin from the back.

Just because you are wrapping around a center doesn't mean you have to make a target. Condense one side and spread the other to make the center off-center. Attach the bud to crinoline with several pins, on the back, to hold the bud until you secure it with stitches.

Tack the center, the perimeter, and as many places in between as are necessary to secure your rows of ribbon. Hide your stitches in the fold of the ribbon. Remove the pin. Trim away the excess crinoline.

See "Layering Crinoline" on pages 120 and 121 to add a ruffled edge to your Hatpin Rose. Add a stamen layer as shown.

Flatbud

Cut a 30 RW length of ribbon (wired only). As in Ruffled Roses (page 31), diagonal down, leaving a ½" tail.

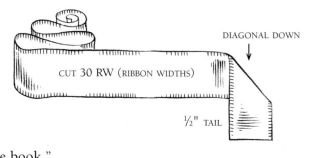

DIAGONAL DOWN

CUT 30 RW (RIBBON WIDTHS)

½" TAIL

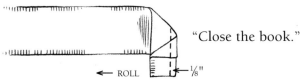

"Close the book."

← ROLL   ⅛"

Start to roll using both hands: one to roll, one to hold. Protect the wire top and bottom. Don't crimp it. Add "air" as you roll, creating ¼"–⅜" gaps between the loops. Your roll will become an oval. Don't squish it. Use up your ribbon.

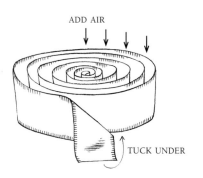

ADD AIR

TUCK UNDER

Set the oval roll onto a circle of crinoline slightly larger than the oval. Diagonal down the end of the ribbon and tuck it under. Reposition the roll. (It can be round without being a target.) Make the center off-center. Flatten the roll with your hand. It probably won't stay down, so hold it down with a duck clip (page 108). Stitch to secure at every turn in the ribbon where a fold can hide your stitch. Stitch inside every corner as shown. Stitch any selvedge showing at the outside edge, disguising your thread in this process. Trim away the excess crinoline.

Opposite page: Detail of child's dress with "cabochon roses" worn by Elena Grimes to perform in a musical trio with her mother and older sister. c. early 1930s. Collection of Holly Gallup.

Cabochon Rosebuds

"At this moment Margarette reappeared wearing a coquettish little night cap with bunches of yellow ribbons technically known as cabbages. She looked ravishing!"

—Dumas, from *Camille*

Various dome-shaped discs of ribbon petals are referred to in vintage texts as "cabochon roses" or "cabbage roses."

Cabochon Rosebud ~ One Rolled Edge

Cut three or four 2 RW lengths of ribbon for the petals. Remove wires. Cut a crinoline circle for the center (diameter = RW)

Knot a separate small length of bud-colored ribbon and tack it to your crinoline.

KNOTTED CENTER

Or coil and tack a much narrower ribbon to your crinoline.

To make the petals, stitch a pin into one corner of each ribbon on the diagonal.

COILED CENTER

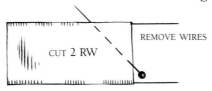

CUT 2 RW   REMOVE WIRES

Fold the ribbon against the pin. Roll up the corner until the raw edges go below the selvedge line. Remove the pin and use it to hold the roll in place.

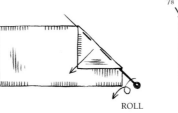

⅛"

ROLL

Stitch as shown.

Draw in slightly to form cup shapes. The diagonal ribbon rolls will face the outside. Attach individually around crinoline. You can add outer petals or ruffles to this rosebud. See "Layering Crinoline" (page 120).

Cabochon Rosebud~
Vintage Classic

For these roses, thinner ribbon works best. Cut three 2 RW lengths of wired or unwired ribbon for your three half-circle petals. Remove wires. Cut a crinoline circle for the center, the same diameter as your ribbon width (diameter = RW).

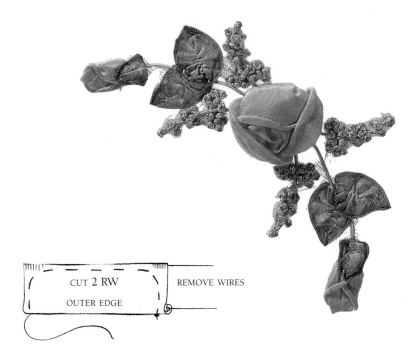

Make a knotted or coiled center as in the previous Cabochon Rosebud. Remember you can place these slightly off-center, the bud might look more natural.

Dampen your first petal piece using water in a spray bottle or pump hair spray. Roll up the outer edge of the ribbon tightly using up one third of your RW. Pin down the ends to hold the roll while drying. Stitch in a half circle as shown. Draw in your stitches (but not too tightly); your petal will cup. Repeat to make the remaining petals. Fit this cupped shape around the crinoline disc and tack on the back. Since the roll is not on the bias, it will fight this process a bit. The petals need to overlap to fit around the bud. You can also make this bud with four petals.

Opposite page: Vintage peignoir and negligees with cabochon rosebuds. c. 1920s. Collection of Jules and Kaethe Kliot of Lacis.

This page: Two flower sprays from 1920s negligee. Collection of Jules and Kaethe Kliot of Lacis.

41

Double Rolled Rosebud

Cut three petals, 2 RW each. Mark midpoint at lower edge. Remove wires. Stitch pins into the two upper corners on the diagonal. Fold the corners against the pins, one toward you and one away.

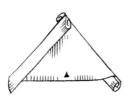

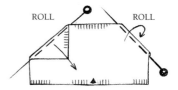

Roll tightly as shown until points overlap (not just touch). Remove the pins and use them to hold the rolls in place at the base. Tack them in place.

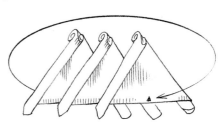

Overlap each triangle petal at the midpoint to form a circle.

Stitch around the base.

Draw in tightly to form a rosebud. Knot to secure. You'll need to cover the base with a calyx with stem (See Index on page 142) or attach a stem wire and cover it with an open Berry Bud or Daffodil Bell (pages 65 and 69).

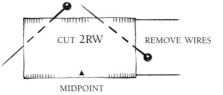

This page and opposite: Vintage variations on the "rolled rosebud" and "dahlia" using diagonally rolled petals of rayon ribbon. Made by Fern Feingut. c. 1950s.

Dahlia

By changing the petal placement and adding more petals, the Double Rolled Rosebud transforms into a Dahlia.

Cut ten to fifteen 2 RW lengths of ribbon. Remove wires. Using diagonal pins as in Double Rolled Rosebud, roll down both edges until a point forms and the rolls compete. You can roll as shown or as in Double Rolled Rosebud.

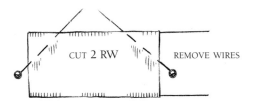

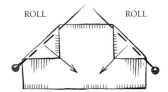

Remove the pins and reuse to hold the rolls in place. Stitch across the lower edge.

The point of each petal will open slightly as you draw in your stitches. Knot to secure if making individually, or work them with a single continuous piece of thread. Place them in a spiral onto crinoline. Add stamens to finish.

43

PETALS

Ribbon flowers are often composed of many petals, be they ruffled rosebuds or crumpled poppies. Sometimes petals act as the fancy, beaded, embroidered and lace-edged collars of your ribbon flower faces, other times they appear with Plain Jane simplicity. Sometimes they are made as separate pieces, other times the ribbon is continuous. Both ways have benefits and drawbacks.

Multi-Petaled Flowers

Some of the most versatile of all the ribbon flowers, the multi-petaled flowers adapt themselves readily to all types and sizes of ribbon. Each multi-petal technique shown is made with a single continuous piece of ribbon. Their petal placement is preordained because they are attached together.

A must for miniature work, these flowers have less bulk than many others, and the raw edges are minimized. They are quick to make and to compose.

When made in miniature, these petaled flowers will create contrast in scale to your larger flowers. Use 4- and 5-Petal Flowers in the same composition. Make them using different colors and sizes. They're the filler flowers of your bouquet, the chorus that fills the stage. If they're blue with yellow centers, they're forget-me-nots. If they're white or yellow, they're the petals of a daffodil. Daffodils have six petals, but I often use five, as it seems less complicated to the eye in ribbonwork.

Opposite page: Contemporary cluster of "multi-petaled flowers" nestles in the folds of a vintage dress accented with embroidery and fagotting. Collection of Brigid Finucane.

This page: Vintage sprays with "5-petal flowers." c. 1920s. Collection of Ruban et Fleur.

45

5-Petal Flower

Cut a 12½ RW length of ribbon. Clean cut across the grain. Fray the edge to insure you are on grain. Trim off the frayed ribbon edge. Use Fray Check or NO FRAY if necessary, especially when working in miniature. Leaving ⅛" allowance at each end, divide your ribbon into five sections (by folding). If you want to be able to distinguish one petal from the next, don't make them too large: 2 or 2½ RW for each petal works well. Any larger and they'll all blend together and look like a continuous ruffle. Mark the outer edge. If you are using wire-edged ribbon, remove the wire from inner edge. Sew a continuous stitch, as shown.

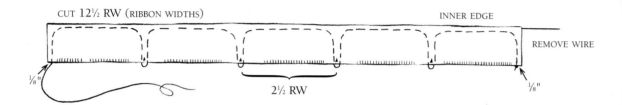

The stitch process is worth noting. It's the same for all of these Multi-Petaled Flowers. Draw your knotted thread through the ribbon, ⅛" from the raw edge, near the selvedge. Backstitch over the selvedge to secure your knot. Stitch as shown, rounding the corners and turning the ribbon in your hand as you continue. Stitch past the marked selvedge at the outer edge. Pull your thread through and reverse the direction of your ribbon. Note the position of your working thread. One of two things will have happened.

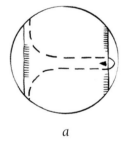

a

a) The thread exited the back. Lift your needle up and over the edge and continue to stitch.

OR

b) The thread exited the front. Bring your needle down and under the edge and continue to stitch.

b

Your thread wraps over the selvedges. This process assures that there will be no logjam when you pull your thread (heavy thread!) to create your petals. When using this technique I'll often draw in the thread after stitching just one petal, to check my stitch size. See "Stitch Lengths" (page 109) for stitch size suggestions.

Continue stitching as shown. Draw in tightly to form the flower center. Backstitch and knot, but don't cut your thread. As complicated as this stitch pattern seems, you'll see it often in the vintage pieces in this book using ¼" or ⅜" ribbon. The same bouquet may have both 4- and 5-Petal Flowers.

To finish off, "make the knots kiss" (pages 17 and 111). The petals may cup when you make this flower. You have a choice; position the cups up or down.

Stitching to crinoline will help stabilize this flower. Stitch around the center, in the folds. Add a center.

Sprays of "5-petal flowers" adorn this sheer textile. Collection of Christine Donough.

47

4-Petal Flower

Cut a 12 RW length of ribbon. Because there are only four, these petals can be slightly larger. Leaving ⅛" allowance, divide your ribbon into four sections. Stitch as in previous 5-Petal Flower.

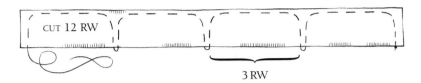

CUT 12 RW

3 RW

3-Petal Flower~In Profile

These petals have a greater size range, 2 to 4 RW. Make your ribbon length calculation accordingly: petal size times three. Stitch as in 5-Petal Flower, but don't make the knots kiss.

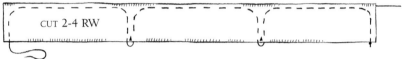

CUT 2-4 RW

Tack your petals to crinoline in a half circle.

Cover with a calyx with stem. (See Index on page 142.) Trim excess crinoline.

2-Petal Flower~Bud or Calyx

Cut a 4 RW length of ribbon. Leaving ⅛" allowance, divide in half. Stitch as in 5-Petal Flower. Fold in half and tack to finish, joining the two petals together.

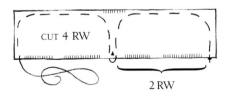

CUT 4 RW

2 RW

If it's green, use it as a calyx. If it's petal colored, add a calyx, stem, and stamens. Let it dangle.

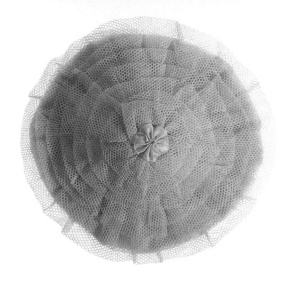

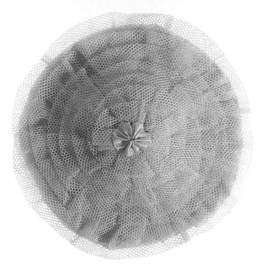

1-Petal

Cut and stitch as shown to create a single petal or bud.

A wide variety of petals can be formed by varying the shape of your stitch pattern. For these petals, you always begin stitching at the edge of your ribbon/fabric. You stitch away from the edge and return to it. Note the changes in shape and proportion. The shape of the stitch pattern effects the shape of the petal. Try incorporating these stitch patterns into the continuous Multi-Petal Flowers. How tightly or loosely you pull in your gathers will also change the look of the finished petal.

HALF OVAL

TRAPEZOID

TRIANGLE

HALF CIRCLE

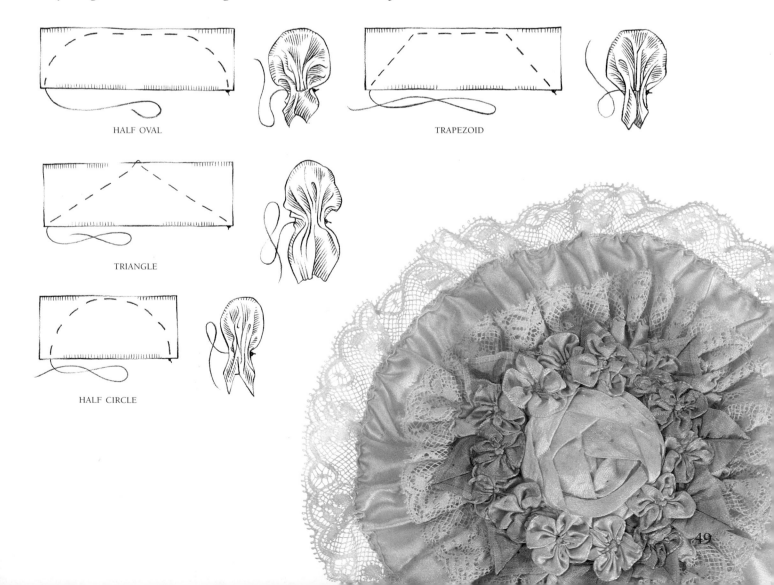

49

Multi-Petal Flower~Twelve Plus

REMOVE WIRE

2-4 RW

Make a longer string of petals, as in the 5-Petal Flower (page 46). Pin to crinoline from the back, then tack in a spiral to create your multi-petaled bloom. I've seen this worked from the center and spiraled outward, or worked from the outer edge then layered inward.

Multi-Petal Flower~ with Mountain Folds

Cut, mark, and follow the stitch pattern as in 4-Petal Flower (page 48). Mark the midpoint of each petal on the outer edge after stitching. Press in mountain folds with an iron (not your fingers). Draw in and finish as in 5-Petal Flower.

MIDPOINT

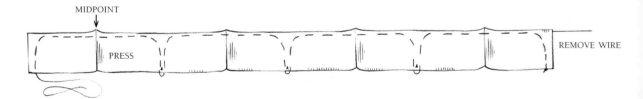

PRESS

REMOVE WIRE

The petals will have a prominent, ridged center spine. You can also apply this technique to other petals in this book.

Multi-Petal Flower~with Tucks

Cut a 15 RW length of ribbon; mark the edges to divide into five sections. Mark the midpoint of each section at the outer edge. Machine stitch the tucks. Now hand stitch as in 5-Petal Flower (page 46). Draw in and finish.

Each petal will have a welted center. You can also apply this technique to other petals in this book.

Multi-Petal Flower~Puffy

The puffy petals of this flower shrink its finished size. For this reason start with a wider ribbon. Cut a 5 RW length of ribbon. Leaving ⅛" allowance at each end, divide into five sections. Stitch as in 5-Petal Flower. Draw in. Your petals will cup. Mount this to crinoline, either with cups up or cups down.

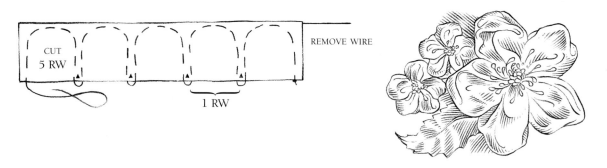

Left: Vintage garter with "4-petal flower." Collection of Arlene Baker.

Knots

Knots are an essential element in ribbonwork. Knotted ribbon buds can peek out from the centers of your flowers. Knotted loops become petals and nests of leaves. Bridal bouquets of the 1920s overflowed with dozens of cascading loops, each worked with a bounty of "love knots."

Pompoms

If you run across one of these on a baby bonnet or christening gown in the bottom of a box or trunk, flattened beyond recognition, don't despair. You can bring it back to life with a hair-curling iron and your shot-of-steam iron, or you can replace it with a new one.

Try 2 yards of ⅛"- ¼"-wide ribbon to start. Satins, acetates, and silks all work well. The silk ribbon for embroidery makes a very tiny knot, which adds contrast to ¼" ribbon. Knot the entire length of ribbon at 2" intervals, leaving a 1" tail at each end.

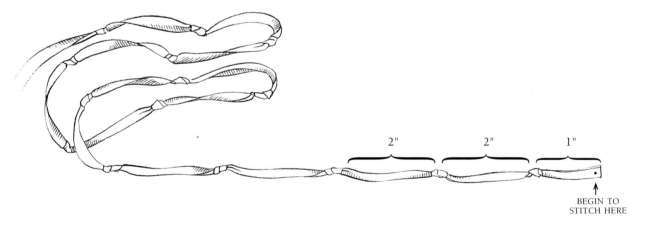

2"   2"   1"

BEGIN TO
STITCH HERE

Draw your needle through the ribbon ⅛" from the cut edge as shown on page 53 and backstitch to secure. Run your needle along the entire length of the ribbon, catching a couple of threads of the weave of the ribbon directly between each set of knots. You don't need 2 yards of thread if you pull as you go along. Be sure to catch the last tail to form the last loop before you draw in tightly. Hold the sandwiched loops between your thumb and index finger, backstitch once through your last loop, and knot off.

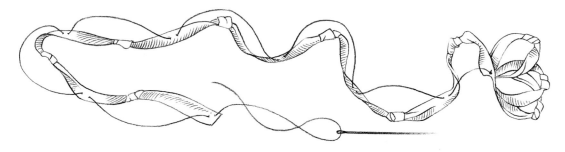

You can make your interval of knots smaller or larger than 2". Measure and cut your tails to half the new intervals. If you go larger, you may need more loops (thus more ribbon) to form its pompom shape. You can also make this flower without knots, stitching at even intervals. Knot some extra ribbon to use for tails, if you wish.

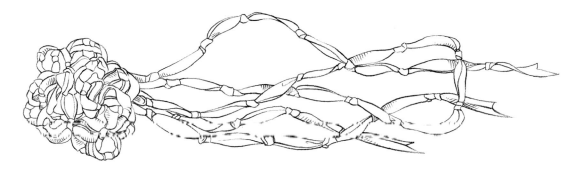

Basic Lazy Daisy

Cut approximately 2 yards of ¼" or smaller ribbon. Stitch at random intervals (2"–4") along the entire length of ribbon. Catch the tail and knot off as in Pompoms. Flatten the loops and arrange them on crinoline, tacking them near the center. Cover with a bud or button. See "Berry Buds, Stamens & Centers" chapter (page 64).

Lazy Daisy~ Knotted

You will need to cut individual petals for this knotted variation. Cut approximately fifteen to twenty-five 2"–4" lengths. Knot each in the center and fold in half.

Tack to crinoline in a circle. Add a center.

Lazy Daisy~ In Profile

Make the profile versions of the Pompom (page 52) or Basic Lazy Daisy by laying your continuous loop or single petals on their side. Tack to crinoline and add a calyx with stem. (See Index on page 142.) You may want to reduce the number of petals.

Knotted M and M's

Use ½" or ⅝"-wide satin ribbon, folded in half and pressed lengthwise, selvedges up. Leaving a 1" tail to begin, make five knots in your ribbon 1½" center to center. Leave a 1" tail at the end and cut the ribbon. As a variation, you might try using a ¼" bias tube, seam side up.

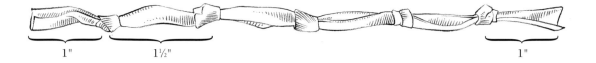

1"   1½"   1"

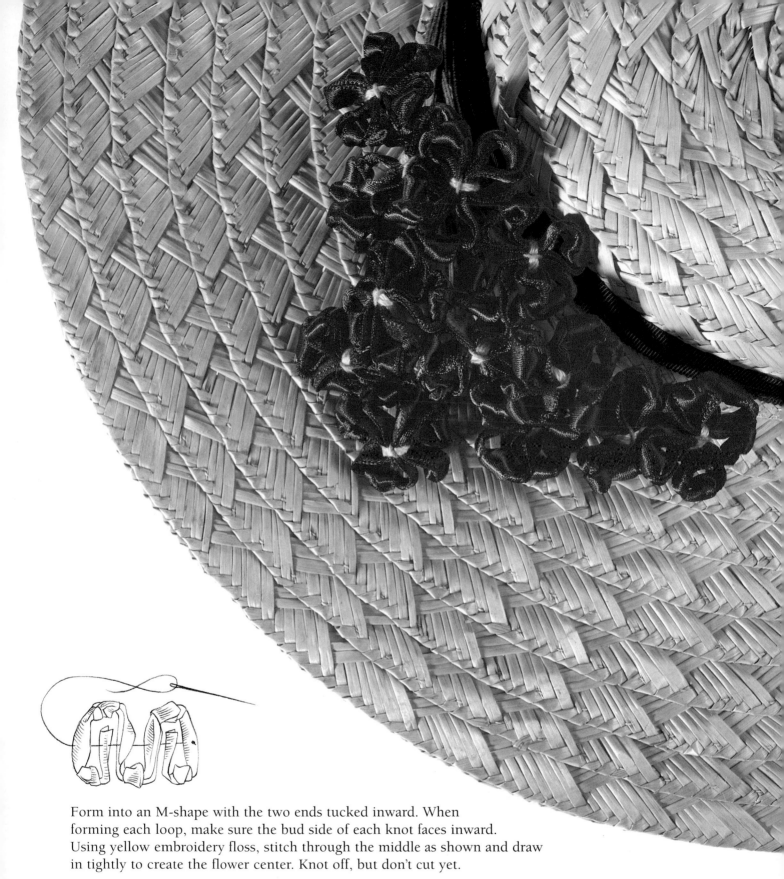

Form into an M-shape with the two ends tucked inward. When forming each loop, make sure the bud side of each knot faces inward. Using yellow embroidery floss, stitch through the middle as shown and draw in tightly to create the flower center. Knot off, but don't cut yet.

Whip around the center several times, then knot off on the fold side (back side). Form the petal shapes on an ironing board with pins. Give the ribbon a strong shot-of-steam and let it cool. Remove the pins and wrap a 12" stem wire across (perpendicular to) your yellow stitches. Draw the two ends of the wire to the back and twist them very tightly several times, close to the flower center, to create a stem.

The golden glow of this vintage straw hat is set off by a cluster of red satin "m and m's." Collection of Candace Kling.

Patt. 1626
25 Meters
Nº 3
Silk, Cotton, Tinsel,
Artificial Silk

MADE IN FRANCE

PANSIES & FUCHSIAS

Pansies

In vintage work, pansies are rarely mixed with other flowers. Instead you'll find them clustered together, in corsage form. They like their own company and are often arranged with bows. There's a logic to this. Pansies have very short stems. You'd hardly expect to see them in a vase with roses or tulips.

To begin, decide which color combination you desire. You have four choices using a single variegated ribbon. Choose one.

UPPER EDGE OF BACK PETALS

LOWER EDGE OF BEARD

Basic Pansy ~ Folded Ribbon

Answer these questions:
What color do you want the upper edges of the back petals?
What color do you want the lower edge of the beard?
You'll use these answers to determine ribbon color placement for your pansy with this technique.

Opposite page: Contemporary "pansies" and "jewel weed" grace this composition of vintage and modern ribbon and leaves. Collections of Meron Reinger, Ruban et Fleur, and Nancy's Sewing Basket.

57

You don't have a choice with the color of the cheeks. They're always the opposite of the beard, because of the way the variegated ribbon is folded.

Start with the back petals. Cut two 4 RW lengths of ribbon. Overlap the ribbons at a right angle and pin diagonally, checking to be sure you have placed your desired color in the correct position. Stitch as shown.

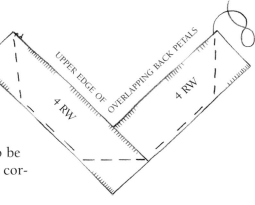

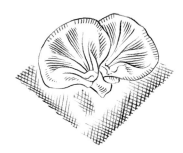

Draw in (not too tightly) so your row of stitches forms a slight arc with a pointed tail in the center as shown. Tack to crinoline close to the gathers, in the folds.

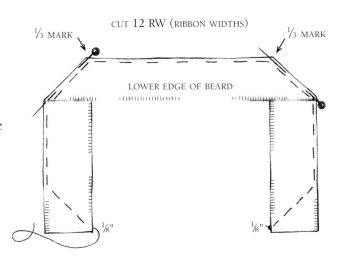

The face of the pansy (cheeks and beard) is folded from a single piece of ribbon. Cut a 12 RW length of ribbon. Divide into thirds by folding. Next, fold as shown, putting pins to hold the diagonals. Notice the position/color of the lower edge of beard.

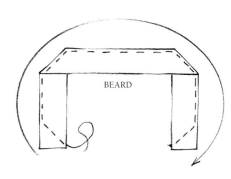

Stitch as shown. Be sure to backstitch over your first knot as you begin. You will need to tug hard on your gathers in order to get a small center. Big stitches will gather smaller. Refer to "Stitch Lengths" (page 109). Try ¼" stitches on 1½" ribbon. The entire stitch pattern condenses to become the center of the pansy.

Draw in your gathers tightly, backstitch over your last stitch, and knot. Don't cut your thread.

"Make the knots kiss" (page 17 and 111). Send your threaded needle back through and beyond your original knot to form a circle. Tug tightly, backstitch, and knot. You want the two petals to meet in a sweetheart shape. There should be a slight (ever so slight) hole in the center when you're done.

Opposite page: A cornucopia of contemporary pansies highlighted by Victorian woven pansy ribbon. Collection of Auralie M. Bradley.

Now you need chrome yellow or chartreuse ribbon for the pansy center. The pansy takes on a different character depending on the size of center you choose. With a large center it looks cartoonish or childlike. With a smaller center it looks more delicate and sophisticated. The choice is yours. Cut 4½" of ⅝" or 1"-wide ribbon. Loop it to form a knot, but don't tighten it. Put your left middle finger (pad side up) into the loop and try to make itty bitty folds across your ribbon. Flatten them with your thumb. Remove your finger and pull the ends of the ribbon to form the knot. It should have ridge lines in it.

Poke the two tails of the knot through the center hole and draw them to the back. Position the fold lines in your knot horizontally.

STITCHED LIKE RAYS OF
THE SUN

Now add the face of your pansy to the crinoline on which you've already stitched your back petals. The crinoline allows you to lower its position. Without it, you'd be tacking your ruffled back petals behind its face. Make your tacking stitches look like little sun rays around the center. They will help position and stabilize your ruffles and secure your center. Hide the stitches in the folds of the ribbon. Knot to secure.

Some pansies have striped veins radiating from their centers. The folds of your gathered ribbon may approximate this. If you choose to embroider these, use DMC #3371, brownish-black rather than black, which may seem harsh. Sometimes the veins are chartreuse or mauve. Change your thread color accordingly to match the veins.

Pansy ~ with a Fancy Face

The three face petals for this pansy are more elaborate due to the addition of a second, narrower ribbon. Cut a 12 RW length of ribbon and fold as in Basic Pansy. To add the second, narrower ribbon, cut three lengths that extend past the diagonal folds ¼" as shown. Consider using rayon hem tape or sheer silk ribbon. Remove any wires. Pin to larger ribbon. Stitch as shown. The extra thickness will require ½" stitches in 1½" ribbon to get a tight center. Complete as in Basic Pansy, adding the center and back petals.

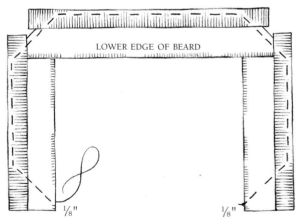

LOWER EDGE OF BEARD

⅛"   ⅛"

Shorten or lengthen any or all of the proportions in this formula to make the "incredible shrinking violet" or its chubby cousin, with more ruffled ears, chubbier cheeks, or a fatter or skinnier beard.

You can use solid ribbon to make pansies, but sometimes you lose the definition of the individual petals. Use a ribbon with a contrasting edge to help accentuate the form.

This double spray of vintage "jewel weed" is a great example of the ice cream colors so popular in the 1920s. Collection of Marianne Reinhold.

Fuchsias

Note the spelling and realize this flower was named after the sixteenth century botanist Leohnard Fuchs. A simplified version of the fuchsia called "jewel weed" appears in a millinery text from 1923. I've seen a hundred of these in a single cluster, all made with soft and lustrous 1920s silk satin baby ribbon. Such objects were called "dainties." In their time, they hung around the boudoir with no purpose other than gratification from sheer beauty. They were the ultimate in frivolous and femmie.

Basic Jewel Weed

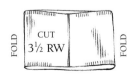

Cut a 3½ RW length of ribbon. Wire removal is optional. Fold the two raw edges to meet at the center. This will be the inside of the bulb. Indent slightly as shown where the corners of the raw edges meet.

Stamen placement varies depending on the size of your ribbon: For 1" and smaller, stagger 3 stamens in the center. Stitch, knot off and cut your thread. For 1½" and larger, stagger 6 stamens at one edge. Whip stitch the stamens at the edge, to secure.

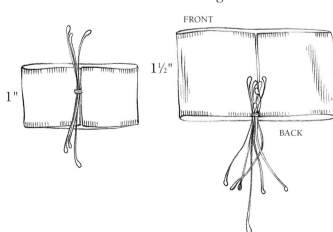

61

When stitching the edges of your diamond, stitch the diamond pattern following the rule for the 5-Petal Flower (page 46). Note the position of the working thread. If it exited at the back, lift the needle up and over the edge. Continue to stitch. If it exited the front, bring the needle down and under the edge. Continue to stitch. Make sure your last stitch goes beyond the first stitch to close the diamond.

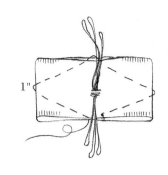
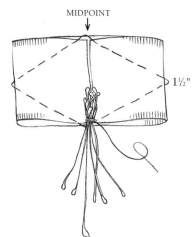

Draw in the gathers of the diamond tightly, backstitch, and knot to secure. You want a cinched waist like Jane Mansfield's. Note that the selvedge of each petal is longer than the fold. The selvedges create the center front curves of your jewel weed or fuchsia.

Introduce a knotted needle up through the center of the bulb and out the top using green (or another color) perle cotton or lightweight cord. This makes the stem on which the flower dangles. Add a long green bead if you like.

Jewel Weed ~ Stuffed

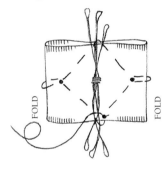

Cut a 2¾ RW length of ribbon. Fold the raw edges to the center as in Basic Jewel Weed and add stamens. Mark the center. Mark two points, each ½ RW from the center. Stitch as shown. Form stuffing into a small ball and place on the center of the ribbon. Draw in your ribbon gathers around the ball and knot to secure. Or wrap your thread several times around the base and then knot.

Fuchsia

The fuchsia has four over-skirt sections drawn up to points. It can have a variety of underskirts, from a totally wild, square-dance petticoat, all white and ruffly, to a more conservative, pen-ciled (tight fitting) wrap-around. Here's the wrap-around underskirt version.

Cut a 3½ RW length of ribbon (wired or unwired) for the overskirt. Fold as in Basic Jewel Weed. Try this first with 1½" or larger ribbon. Now you need to add your underskirt. You will need a ribbon half the size of the overskirt ribbon. You can trim a wider ribbon, if necessary. The raw edge will be tucked inside the bulb.

Cut a 3 RW length of ribbon for the underskirt. Whip stitch stamens at midpoint of underskirt, staggered as shown. Fuchsia stamens are like lovely long dancers' legs, but one fancy slipper hangs longer.

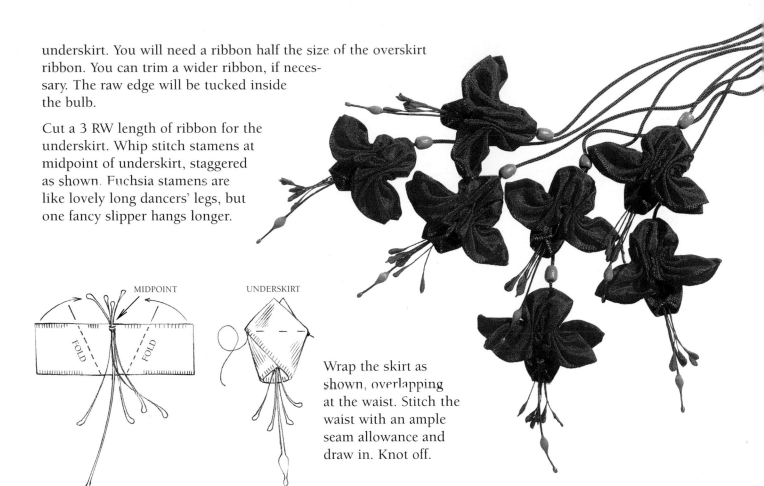

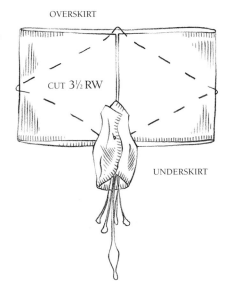

Wrap the skirt as shown, overlapping at the waist. Stitch the waist with an ample seam allowance and draw in. Knot off.

Tack the underskirt with one stitch to your overskirt as shown. Stitch and finish off as in Basic Jewel Weed (page 61). When stitching your diamond pattern, avoid catching the underskirt. Stitch on the wider ribbon only. As you finish off, be sure you've stitched past your beginning stitch to close the gap. Add a stem as in Basic Jewel Weed.

Left: Vintage fuchsia stamens with dewdrop tips. Collection of Ruban et Fleur.

BERRY BUDS, STAMENS & CENTERS

Is it a berry, a bud, a stamen, or a flower center?
The techniques to make them are often used interchangeably.
Color and placement will define their role.

Berry Buds

Sometimes berry buds stand alone, sometimes they're inside flowers, sometimes they peek from behind petals, and sometimes they're on stems. Often they nestle together in clusters. There can be a humorous quality about them. Stitch them slightly off center to give perspective and movement to your work.

Basic Berry Bud

If you're using variegated ribbon, you need to make a decision about color. In most instances you'll only see half the ribbon on the finished bud, unless you're mounting it on a stem.

Cut a 3 RW length of ribbon. Remove wires. Important at any time, but crucial in miniature, is cutting the ribbon on grain. Cut across the ribbon as straight as you can. This will not guarantee that you are on grain. Pull out any loose threads and recut if needed. Use Fray Check or NO FRAY if necessary. Stitch raw edges together with ⅛" seam to make a tube.

Opposite page: Double-ended stamens in bales, as they arrive from the manufacturer. Courtesy of Jules and Kaethe Kliot of Lacis.

65

OVERLAPPING FOLD

CUT 3 RW (RIBBON WIDTHS)

Miniature flowers often don't require miniature seams. Even if you're working with ribbon as tiny as ⅝" you still make an ample seam. It's important that you catch both selvedges as you stitch and that your thread matches. Turn the seam to the inside. As you place seams to one side, carefully cover the seamline with an overlapping fold. This will hide/cover any stress to the ribbon caused by your stitches. Finger press this seam using your "milliner's shot-of-steam" (page 54).

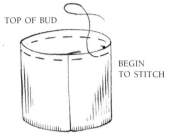

TOP OF BUD

BEGIN TO STITCH

Refer now to "Circular Stitching" (page 110). Start at a random spot along the selvedge edge when you introduce your threaded needle. Avoid beginning on the seam. Your stitches will glide past the seam more easily, to meet and overtake slightly, your first knot. If your stitches are too tiny, you won't be able to tighten the hole. See "Stitch Lengths" and "Quilters' Challenge" (page 109).

TOP FIRST

Draw in your stitches to close the bud. Hold it closed as you back-stitch and then knot. It will be easier to stitch the top tightly before the bud is stuffed. On the bottom of the bud you'll be knotting under tension, which is more difficult. Stitch the bottom in the same way as the top. Leave the needle dangling, so you are ready to complete the next step.

Cradle the cup in your slightly closed hand, pushing a substantial amount of polyester or cotton batting down into the cup. Draw in your stitches as you did for the top, backstitch, and knot. Because it's the back, you don't need to be as careful about it. You already did a good job on the front. Remember, if it doesn't show, it doesn't count.

If done with thicker ribbon, the stitches will create gathers that form deep grooves/indentations in the berry bud. The shape is not going to be as rounded. That's not a negative, it's just different. Also, you may need larger stitches due to the thickness of the ribbon.

Berry Bud ~ Colored Center

Opposite page: Contemporary "berry buds" with metallic lace ruffle accents. Ribbons courtesy of Paulette Knight.

Proceed as in Basic Berry Bud. Draw in your stitches for the top of the bud. Leave a small hole, ³⁄₁₆"–¼". Place a ½" circle of contrasting fabric over the hole on the inside before you stuff. No need to stitch it, the stuffing will hold it in place. Insert stuffing and finish as in Basic Berry Bud.

Berry Bud ~ Ruffled Top

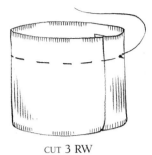

CUT 3 RW

The row of stitching at the top of the bud doesn't kiss the selvedge in this variation. Start ⅙ to ¼ of the way down from the edge to create a ruffle that sticks out. Proceed as in Basic Berry Bud (page 65) letting your raw seam allowances show at the center of this bud. Use Fray Check or NO FRAY to stablize them.

Berry Bud ~ Lace Ruffle

Add a lace ruffle, top or bottom, facing in or facing out. Cut your ribbon and stitch your lace to it while it's still flat. You can use your sewing machine for this stitching. Proceed as in Basic Berry Bud (page 65). You will still be stitching near the selvedge edges to form the bud.

LACE FACING OUT

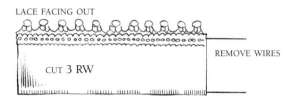

CUT 3 RW

REMOVE WIRES

LACE FACING IN

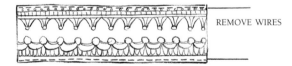

REMOVE WIRES

Berry Bud ~ with Stem

Mount any of your berry buds on stem wire, if desired. Attach the stems after you've finished the top, and before you've drawn in the bottom. Make a small loop in the top of the stem wire. Tack to the top of the bud on the inside. Stuff around it. Draw the back of the bud down around the wire, backstitch, and knot.

Berry Bud ～ Daffodil Bell

It's just a short step from Berry Bud—Ruffled Top, to the daffodil bell. The daffodil bell is an unstuffed berry bud with a loosely gathered top, but it requires a bit more ribbon.

When making a daffodil, use the same width ribbon for the petals and the bell. Make your petals first. See 5-Petal Flower (page 46).

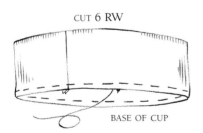

CUT 6 RW

BASE OF CUP

To make the bell, cut a 6 RW length of ribbon (wired or unwired). Fray to straighten the grain and cut again. Use Fray Check or NO FRAY. If using wire-edged ribbon, remove wire from what will be the base of the cup. Stitch the raw edges together with an ⅛" seam. Turn right side out. Finger press the seam to the side. Stitch around the base.

Draw in tightly. Stay on your needle and attach the open cup to the center of the petals. To stabilize the base of the cup to the petals, make your stitches like spokes of a wheel around the center.

Stitch around the top of your cup, ⅛"–³⁄₁₆" down from the upper edge, to create the ruffle of the daffodil bell. Avoid beginning at the seam when doing this. See "Circular Stitching" (page 110).

Draw in the gathers as much or as little as seems balanced to your taste. If you keep the wire in the top of the cup, the gathers won't magically form into beautiful little fluted folds. You'll need to work the top edges to get them to form a more elaborate scrolled effect. See "Picking and Poking" (page 100).

The formula 6 RW isn't etched in stone. A little more or less will alter the amount of ruffle and the plumpness of the cup. In miniature, and in blue, this cup might be a blue bell. In green it could be a calyx.

Wrapped Berry Buds

You can use ribbon if you have the right width available, but this series of wrapped buds, especially when larger, is often done with fabric. Sometimes these buds nest among the petals to form the centers of flowers, sometimes they stand alone, but usually they nest in clusters.

Basic Wrapped Berry Bud

Form cotton into a tight ball with your fingers, around the end of a stem wire or cord. Measure the ball to obtain its circumference. Cut a circle of fabric/ribbon whose diameter equals this measurement plus ¼". The formula is diameter = circumference + ¼". Using green floss, stitch around the circumference of this circle. Draw the circle in around your stuffing until it is tight against your stem wire or cord. Knot but don't cut. Wrap the green floss around the base to secure, then continue wrapping the floss to create a calyx.

Vintage cluster on vertical bow with "wrapped fabric buds." Collection of Jules and Kaethe Kliot of Lacis.

FABRIC CIRCLE

DIAMETER OF FABRIC = CIRCUMFERENCE + ¼"

Wrapped Berry Bud ~ Segmented

This bud has a center filled with a bead or stuffing. Measure around it to obtain the circumference. Cut the ribbon or fabric using this measurement. Don't add seam allowances to this measurement. Stitch as in Basic Wrapped Berry Bud. On this variation, when drawing in the circle, the raw edges butt at the center back. Knot and cut your thread.

This bud often has a squashed look. If you want this look, come up through the center and back down again, catching a couple of threads of the weave on top as you do this. Hold the bud between your thumb and index finger as you draw down the thread to the desired height.

To segment your bud, use a decorative thread such as buttonhole twist or perle cotton. Insert the needle up through the center, pulling the thread through as you come out the top. Draw the thread around the outside edge of the bud. Repeat the process to form each spoke of the wheel. Catch your last stitch at center back and knot off.

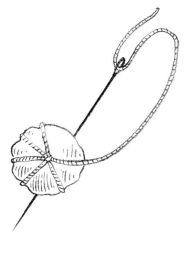

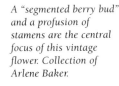

A "segmented berry bud" and a profusion of stamens are the central focus of this vintage flower. Collection of Arlene Baker.

Wrapped Berry Bud ~ Dimpled Bead

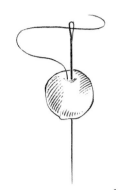

Use a bead this time and proceed as in Basic Wrapped Berry Bud. Draw your circle of fabric down over your bead.

Secure with a knot, but don't cut your thread. Form the dimple by inserting your needle at center back where raw edges converge. Put the needle up through the hole in the bead, pulling the thread through as you come out the top. To form the dimple, insert the needle back down through the center of the bead. Move your needle over several threads of the weave to avoid going back down through your original hole. Pull the thread slightly taut and knot off.

Vintage powder puff wand with stamens set under berry center. c. 1920s. Collection of Arlene Baker.

Stamens

Stamens bring the ribbon to life. Adding stamens transforms what was a ruffle into a bloom. The density of ribbon, both its texture and its color, may be offset by the use of stamens. Adding a few may look airy and dance-like, while a mass will seem fuller and more fertile. Consider whether you want to nest the stamens or position them to look long and graceful like a dancer's legs. The moods are quite different; one safe and secure, the other a bit wilder.

The Mystery Dance

Both single- and double-ended stamens are available in a wide range of colors and shapes. Venture beyond the common white pearlized ones. Golden yellows to oranges should be staples in your stamen collection, yet always look to nature for some surprising answers. Occasionally you might consider mixing yellow stamens with green ones. Rarely are stamens the same color as the flower. They are more often brightly colored, in extreme contrast to the flower. Stamens are nature's invitation to the mystery dance.

Stamen Etiquette

To take stamens from the bundle, first hold your stamen bundle and untwist the wire around it. Take out as many as you need. *Put the wire back on.* Hold the beginning of the wire under your thumb, against the center of the bundle. Wrap the wire in a tight spiral around your stamens. That's all. *Don't twist the wire.* The wire will eventually break after repeated twisting and the shorter piece won't hold your bundle.

Introducing Stamens

Choose your desired amount of stamens. Bundle them in the center with wire or thread. If using wire, crimp it over the stamens. Twist to secure.

TWIST

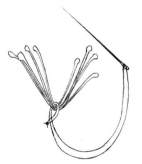

If using thread, knot your needle with double thread. Loop it around your stamens and draw the needle through between the threads at the knotted end. Tighten the thread around your stamen bundle.

Use your threaded needle to sew your stamens in place. Placement of the stamens differs from flower to flower. Sometimes your stamens are stitched to the front of the flower and sometimes they are folded in half and drawn partially through to the back.

To mount stamens behind a miniature flower, fold them in half, then in half again. Stamens are rarely cut, even if they are too long and would hang over the edge of the flower. Stamens cut in half (even if stitched down) will slip out over time, especially when coaxed by an inquisitive hand. The stamens are doubled back on themselves (folded) instead.

73

Buds, Not Stamens

Sometimes what looks like a stamen isn't. If the ends are green with colored tips, or the tip is cupped in two calyx-like petals, you've got miniature buds. These buds are made to peek or dangle from the edges of your baby flowers. Another indication is that their connecting thread is green like a stem.

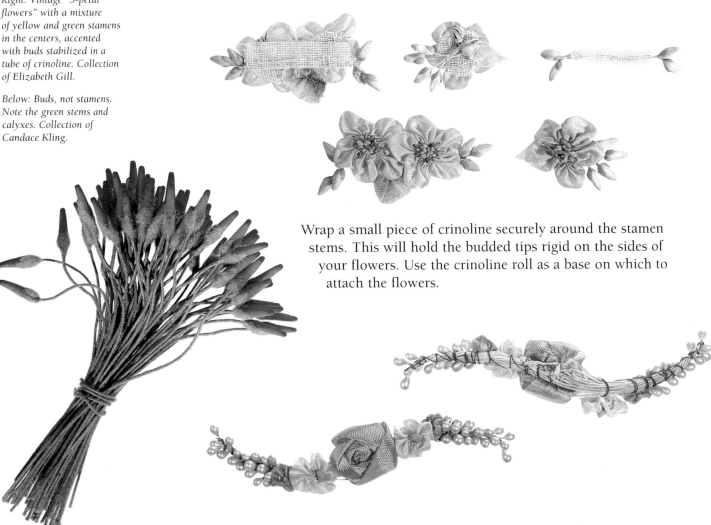

Wrap a small piece of crinoline securely around the stamen stems. This will hold the budded tips rigid on the sides of your flowers. Use the crinoline roll as a base on which to attach the flowers.

Centers

In "Rosebuds" (starting page 36) you'll find a variety of flower bud centers made from ribbons that have been knotted, twisted, spiraled and stitched. There are also some tips on petal placement. Introduce these buds, or the buttons and fringe described here, into your ribbon flowers.

Buttons

Use buttons as centers for your flowers. Vintage buttons will help create a vintage feel in your work. Celluloid ones will look more Art Deco, steel-cut more Victorian. They also serve to cover raw edges, unsightly knots, frayed ribbon, or a too-large hole. You'll need a touch of crinoline behind to secure them.

Below: Vivid colored fringed centers call out from these vintages roses. Their calyxes are open-ended variations on the "berry bud." c. 1950s. Made by Fern Feingut.

Fringed Centers

FOLD   ROLL

Cut off the selvedges of your ribbon. Fringe both sides.

Fold in half lengthwise and roll up. Secure with a stitch.

You can custom cut your ribbon to the appropriate size by trimming more off one edge.

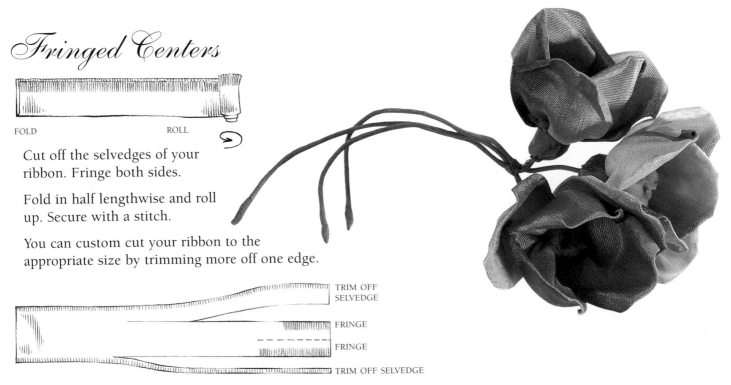

TRIM OFF SELVEDGE

FRINGE

FRINGE

TRIM OFF SELVEDGE

GREEN

Green creates the background that makes your ribbon flowers stand out. Every ribbon flower bouquet deserves to be accented by gracefully dancing leaves. Leaves add movement to your work. They are the fingertips of your ribbon dance. Enhance your corsage with a scrunchy green ruffle, handfuls of miniature green ribbon points, or several large ruffle-edged leaves. Leaves don't need to lie flat like a halo around and behind your flowers. Let them reach out from between them. As you study the following examples, notice that many ribbon leaf and petal forms are interchangeable. If it's green it's a leaf (or perhaps a calyx); if it's pink it's a petal or bud.

Opposite page: Packets of vintage velvet leaves in their original shipping container. Collection of Ruban et Fleur.

Right: A sheer green ribbon with the tiniest of stripes accents this bud and bow combination. c. 1920s. Collection of Jules and Kaethe Kliot of Lacis.

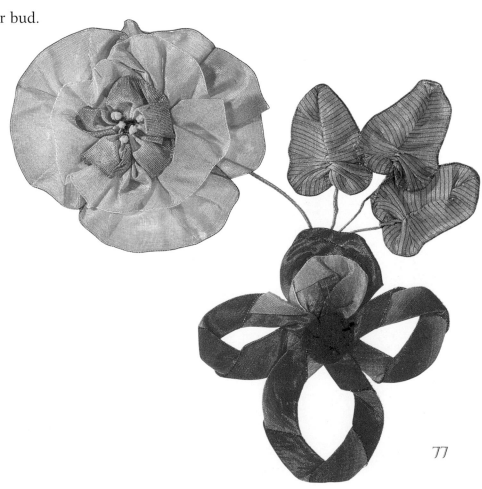

1920s Leaf

A 1920s standard, this simple leaf's appearance is more rounded at the tip than its boat-shaped cousin. Its overall appearance is more oval.

1920s Leaf

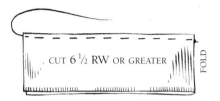

Cut a 6½ RW length of ribbon (or greater). Fold the ribbon in half crosswise. Start stitching at the fold, backstitching to secure your knot. Take ⅛"–¼" stitches along the entire edge of what will be the spine of your leaf.

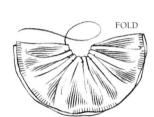

When you reach the end, draw in your stitches and backstitch to secure. Don't cut your thread. You will use it to continue stitching.

If using unwired ribbon, use especially large stitches (¼"), so the selvedges will appear down the center of your leaf and form little ridges. If you want your unwired ribbon leaves to hold their shape, try stitching with beading wire instead of thread.

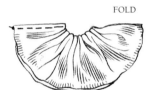

Continue stitching, this time along the two raw edges. When you reach the selvedge, knot off and cut your thread (don't draw in this section).

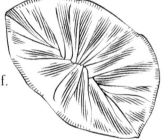

Open your leaf.

Boat Leaves

This is an extremely versatile leaf, more pointed than some, but easily customized, longer, shorter, narrower, ruffled, pleated, with or without a stem. It looks equally good wired or unwired, in velvet, satin, or grosgrain ribbon.

Basic Boat Leaf

Cut a 7-12 RW length of ribbon. If you cut the ribbon longer, the width of the leaf will remain the same, but the leaf will be longer and more ruffly. Fold the ribbon in half crosswise.

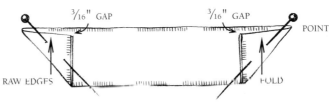

Fold up the two corners of the ribbon as shown to form a boat shape. Form points at the tips of the diagonal folds.

Now overturn your boat! It will be easier to stitch. Begin stitching at the end with the original crosswise fold. Start ⅛" from the point, close to the diagonal fold. Two-thirds of the way along the diagonal, backstitch and then continue stitching.

Draw your gathers into the bottom of the boat. The backstitch will stop them. Smooth out the back of the leaf. Open the leaf to check on the desired size, and knot the thread where you finished stitching when you are satisfied.

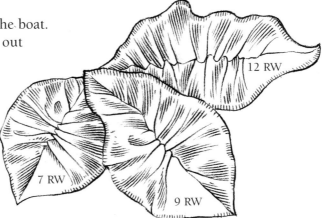

Boat Leaf ~ with Stem

Add your boat leaf measurement to twice your stem length, then cut this length of ribbon (wired only). Fold the ribbon in half crosswise. Measuring in from the raw edges, mark the stem length as shown. Fold and pin the diagonal fold of the front of the boat. Stitch as shown in the Basic Boat Leaf (inverting your boat). Draw in the gathers. Knot the thread and cut.

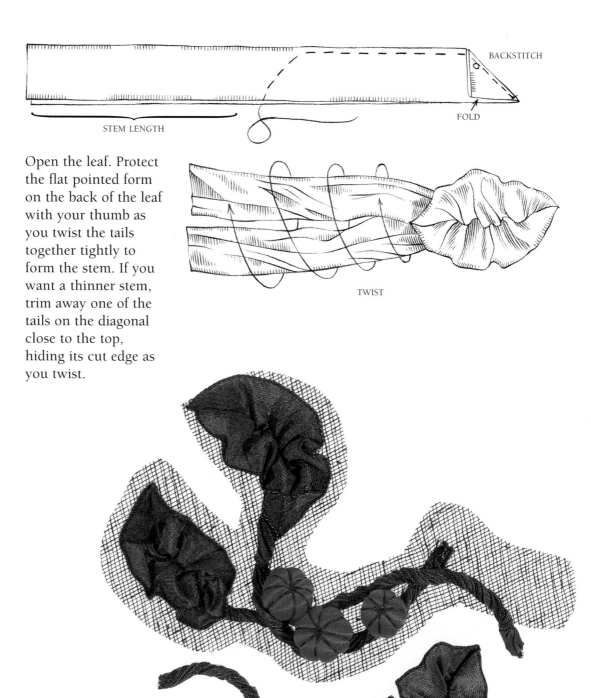

BACKSTITCH

STEM LENGTH

FOLD

Open the leaf. Protect the flat pointed form on the back of the leaf with your thumb as you twist the tails together tightly to form the stem. If you want a thinner stem, trim away one of the tails on the diagonal close to the top, hiding its cut edge as you twist.

TWIST

Boat Leaf~ Folded Ribbon

DOUBLE RUFFLED EDGE

NEW
RW

FOLD IN HALF

DOUBLE SELVEDGE EDGE

NEW
RW

FOLD SO BOTH SELVEDGES SHOW

RUFFLED SPINE

NEW
RW

FOLD TO CREATE RUFFLED SPINE

Fold the ribbon lengthwise. The position of your fold will change the look of the finished leaf.

Fold ribbon (wired only) exactly in half (selvedges on *top* of each other) and separate the wired edges to create a double ruffly leaf when your stitching is completed.

OR

Fold with selvedges right *next* to one another (use ombre/variegated for this) to create a contrasting stripe at the outer edge of your finished leaf.

Fold a quarter to a third of your ribbon to create a ruffle down the spine of your leaf.

Remember it is your new folded width that becomes the ribbon width (RW) for your leaf formula. Now fold in half, turn up the diagonals, and stitch all the variations as in Basic Boat Leaf.

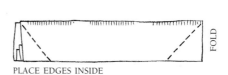

FOLD

PLACE EDGES INSIDE

Boat Leaf~ Separate Ruffled/Pleated Spine

Cut and fold as in Basic Boat Leaf. Pin the diagonals. Insert a separate, narrower, pleated, or gathered ribbon into the bottom of your boat, *inside, between the two ribbon layers.* This ribbon could be another color. Stitch as in Basic Boat Leaf. When you open your leaf it will have a separate, more intensely ruffled spine.

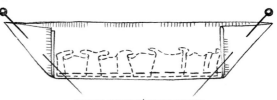

INSERT RUFFLE/PLEAT INSIDE,
BETWEEN TWO RIBBON LAYERS

Boat Leaf ~ Customized Width

If you only have a wide ribbon, but you want a narrow leaf, stitch the ribbon in further from the edge. The excess will be hidden on the back. You will have to plan the new width ahead of time to use when cutting your ribbon length.

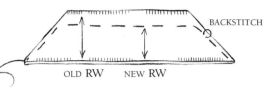

BACKSTITCH

OLD RW   NEW RW

Boat Leaf ~ Asymmetrical with Gathers

This leaf has more gathers on one side than the other and it curves in one direction. Do a mirror image of the illustration, and the leaf will curve the other way.

Cut a 10½ RW length. Fold as shown with a 3½ RW tail.

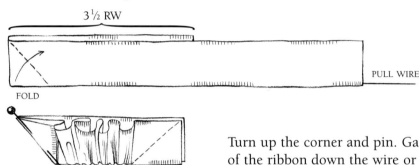

3½ RW

PULL WIRE

FOLD

SMOOTH

Turn up the corner and pin. Gather the long portion of the ribbon down the wire or by stitching until the two raw edges meet. Smooth the end so you can turn up the second corner and pin.

Overturn your boat. Stitch as in Basic Boat Leaf.

BACKSTITCH

OVERTURN TO STITCH

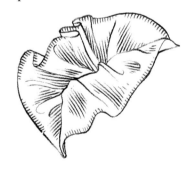

Boat Leaf ~ Asymmetrical with Pleats

This leaf has many pleats on one side and is smooth on the other. It curves in one direction. Make a mirror image of the illustration and the leaf will curve the other way.

Cut an 11½ RW length (wired only). Fold as shown, leaving a 3½ RW tail. Turn up the corner and pin.

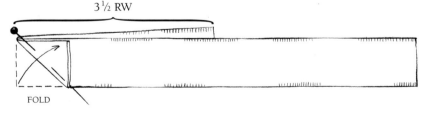

3½ RW

FOLD

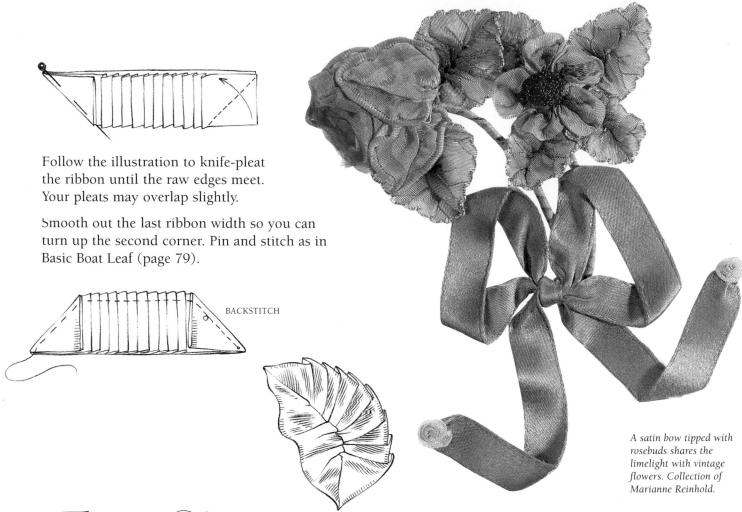

Follow the illustration to knife-pleat the ribbon until the raw edges meet. Your pleats may overlap slightly.

Smooth out the last ribbon width so you can turn up the second corner. Pin and stitch as in Basic Boat Leaf (page 79).

BACKSTITCH

A satin bow tipped with rosebuds shares the limelight with vintage flowers. Collection of Marianne Reinhold.

Folded Leaves

Many leaves are folded to create their pointed tips. If you're making folded buds with the following techniques some of which are coat-like, you don't have to fold them with pointed pencil necks. There's room for variation. The mood of your work will change according to your choice. Pointed buds with small necks have a hard-edged look. They look predatory. They convey that your rose might have thorns. In the 1920s many of the buds had very wide necks. This gave them a gentle and soft quality. Even their stamens were blunted and tucked inside.

Basic Man in His Kimono

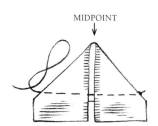

MIDPOINT

Cut a 2½ RW length for each leaf/petal. Remove wire from the lower edge. Diagonal down the two edges to form a point, or as a vintage text commands, "make a right-hand bias and a left-hand bias." If you have wire in the lapels of his kimono, be sure it's neat and even without crimps. Stitch the base/waist, catching the selvedge in the back.

Draw in your stitches tightly and knot off. Your wired lapels become the spine, which can then be easily shaped, but even without wire, this leaf/petal/bud has a pleasing look.

Man in His Kimono~ Long Lapels

With this variation you'll have long lapels to twist to form a stem. Measure a 2½ RW length plus twice the stem length before cutting your ribbon (wired only). Fold and stitch as in Basic Man in His Kimono. Twist the tails to form the stem. The wires in the ribbon help to hold your twisted stem in place. You might succeed using unwired ribbon if you stitch the stem immediately to a backing.

Above and below right: Vintage flower clusters, petals and buds made with variations on the "man in his kimono." Collection of Jules and Kaethe Kliot of Lacis.

A happy accident occurs if you make this leaf with a variegated ribbon that blends from green to rose. This will transform your leaf into a budded calyx on a stem.

Man in His Kimono ~ Budded Center

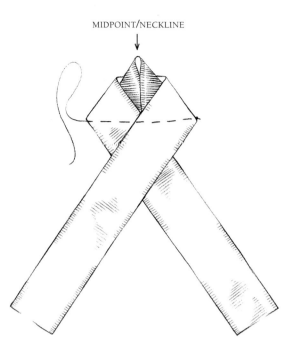

MIDPOINT/NECKLINE

Cut one 2½ RW bud-colored piece and fold as in Basic Man in His Kimono (page 83). Cut a second leaf-colored piece as in Man in His Kimono—Long Lapels (wired only). Both ribbons should be the same width. Wrap the longer ribbon around the shorter one. Notice that the ribbon gaps at the neckline if you make it meet at the waist. What will be the stem also overlaps below the waist. Pin the waistline to secure. Catch the back waist and bud tails in this process. Stitch.

Pull the thread down tightly and knot off. Twist tails to form stem. To reduce bulk, trim away one of the tails, as in Boat Leaf–With Stem (page 80).

Basic Man Overlapping His Coat

Cut a 3½ RW length for each leaf/petal/bud.

MIDPOINT

CUT 3½ RW

MIDPOINT

Find the midpoint of your ribbon. Overlap 60°, or in thirds, to form the bud. This would be like overlapping your coat over each hip.

Stitch across, catching the back selvedge.

Or stitch slightly lower avoiding it.

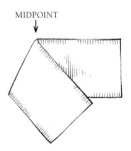

Draw in your stitches and knot off. Instead of stitching, you might try gathering the ribbon with your fingers and feeding little pleats of ribbon from one set of fingers into the other. Train your hands to gather without needle and thread. Keep holding and wrap with wire to secure.

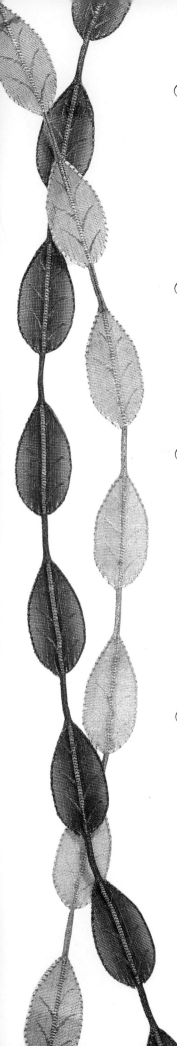

Man Overlapping His Coat ~ with Lapel

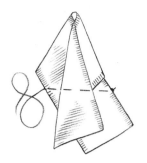

Cut and fold as in Basic Man Overlapping His Coat. Turn the last selvedge back to create the lapel. Stitch as in Basic Man Overlapping His Coat. When made with green ribbon, the lapel creates the spine of your leaf.

Man Overlapping His Coat ~ Shawl Collar

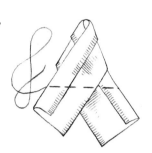

Cut a 3 RW length. Turn one selvedge back on itself, ¼ – ⅙ RW. Fold and stitch as in Basic Man Overlapping His Coat.

Man Overlapping His Coat ~ Calyx with Stem

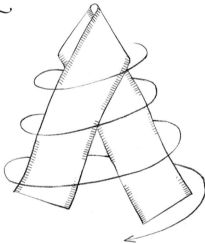

This leaf with stem becomes a calyx when you add petals.

Measure 3 RW plus twice your stem length and cut your ribbon (wired only). Find the midpoint and make the overlaps. Gathering with your hands, not thread, draw the base of the point together in your fingers. Hold in one hand. Don't let go. With your other hand twist the tails tightly to form the stem.

Man Overlapping His Coat ~ Budded Center

Using bud-colored ribbon, cut a 3 RW length, then fold as in Basic Man Overlapping His Coat, but don't stitch. Using leaf-colored ribbon the same width as the first ribbon (wired only) will give the bud a green coat, overlapping, with long lapels. Note that the green ribbon gaps at the neckline. Stitch across the lowered waistline. Be sure to catch the bud tails in the back as well as the green selvedge edges. Larger stitches will condense smaller.

Vintage leaf trims of woven metallic with wired spines. Collection of Candace Kling.

Draw your stitches in tightly and make a backstitch. Send your needle to the back in a fold to hide it, then knot off. Twist the tails to form the stem.

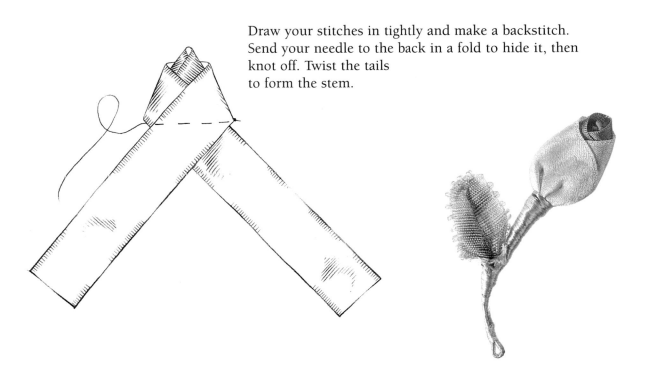

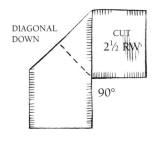

House Leaves

This leaf is simple, dimensional, and easily made in miniature. The raw edge is minimal. You could form it with ribbon as narrow as ¼". There's very little stitching involved. This leaf is most successful with a short piece of ribbon, because a long piece, 4 RW or greater, will not create the same dramatic cupping effect.

Basic House Leaf

Try this leaf in paper first to perfect your technique. Cut a 2½ RW length. Fold as shown, on the diagonal (diagonal down).

DIAGONAL DOWN

CUT 2½ RW

90°

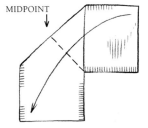

MIDPOINT

Note the dotted line from the midpoint of the fold to the corner point. Fold on this line.

Now it looks like a child's drawing of a house.

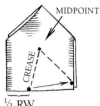

MIDPOINT

CREASE

⅓ RW

One side has a roof line, the other side is plain. Work on the plain side. Mark the midway point at your roof line. Mark ⅓ RW at the floor line of your house (the raw edge). Using your finger, crease from the ⅓ mark to the midpoint.

Following the arrow, bring your fold over to the selvedge edge to form a dart, cupping the leaf. Note especially that the seam allowances do not line up. You are folding slightly off center, aiming toward the point of the leaf (your bottom edges don't line up).

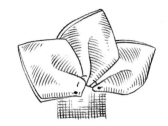

Make several leaves at the same time. Don't pin them, hold them with duck clips (page 108). Stitch these leaves, in a fan shape, to crinoline by machine or by hand.

House Leaf ~ Leaf / Calyx with Stem

CUT 12 RW

90° FOLD TO FORM A WASHINGTON MONUMENT SHAPE

A leaf with a stem can become a calyx if petals are added. Cut a 12 RW length (wired only) and form the ribbon as in Basic House Leaf.

Create a dart near the top as in Basic House Leaf, then twist the tails to form the stem.

FOLD, THEN TWIST

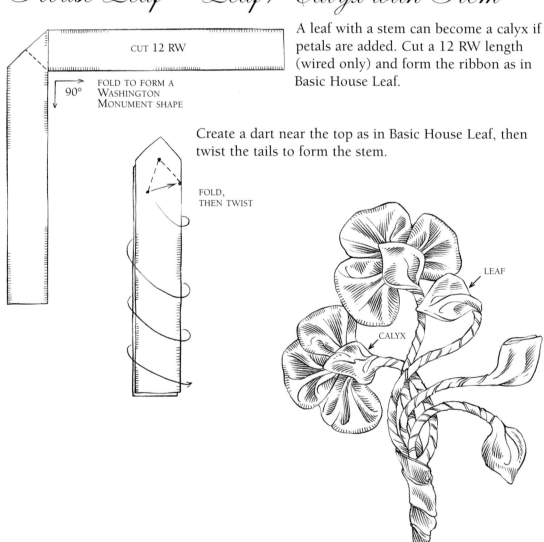

LEAF

CALYX

Puffy Wired Leaf

This leaf has more of the look of fabric than ribbon, as its outer edge is on the fold rather than the selvedge. It has a great curved profile. If you pull the wire out by mistake while doing this technique, give it up and cut a new piece of ribbon. If your ribbon starts to fray, see "Frayed Selvedge" (page 114).

When first learning, try using 1½" ribbon. Cut a 7 RW length (wired only). At one end of the ribbon pull both wires out 1½". Fold the ribbon in half so the wires meet. Open the ends of the wire as shown, like scissors, and twist them around each other several times.

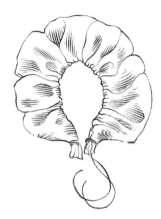

Condense the fold of ribbon with your fingers, and wrap the wires around the fold.

At the opposite end of the ribbon, pull each of the wires down until the ribbon is condensed to approximately 3". The various weaves of ribbon produce different degrees of gather. When you get one wire done, crimp the wire to hold it temporarily Pull down the second wire to match the first wire. Check to see that both sides are gathered equally.

Finish off this second set of wires as you did the first. Now the beginning and the end look the same. Crimp the top of the loop to draw the gathered selvedges together to form the spine of the leaf. Bring both ends together to form a loop, wrapping them with the remaining wires.

Working from the back, slip stitch the selvedges together. The gathered selvedges on the back can be left open. Spread the outside edge of the leaf where the ruffle has hidden itself in its own folds.

"Boat leaves" ring this vintage rose constructed with sheer rolled petal edges. Collection of Deborah Starks.

Scrunchy Leaves

Not all greenery is perceivable leaves. Some greenery is backdrop or foliage. It wraps its way around a flower, or wends its way past several or throughout a whole bouquet. It's going to look like foliage even though you can't actually spot or pick out a leaf, just green ruffles tucked in.

The "Scrunched" ribbon described in "Textured Finishes" chapter (page 98) works wonderfully for these leaves. You can form the scrunched ribbon into leaf shapes if you wish, or leave it in its more random form as a ruffled lettuce edge.

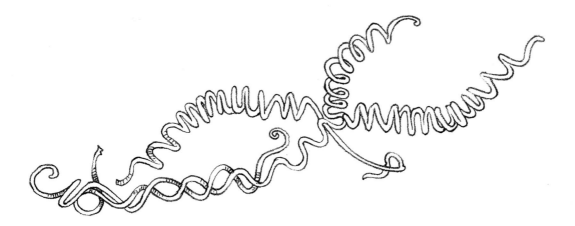

Tendrils

Tendrils are like stems, but without a leaf, bud, or flower finish. Tendrils contain the energy of new life, coiled and ready to spring. They can convey humor, intensity, or a degree of wildness.

Most commonly used for tendrils is stem wire of various gauges, wrapped around a pencil or narrower round object. It comes in green or white and is available at most craft and floral supply stores. You may need Fray Check or NO FRAY or a dab of glue to secure the threads at the tips.

You might also try the various gauges of beading wire in brass or silver, or the electrical wires that are plastic coated and come in a variety of bright colors.

Stems

A variety of materials will work as stems. It's a matter of finding a material that is compatible in color and size.

❋ NARROW GREEN RIBBON—tacked down.

❋ WIRE-EDGED RIBBON—twisted tightly. Different widths of ribbon will create different thicknesses of stems.

❋ VARIEGATED OMBRE WIRE-EDGED RIBBON—twisted to favor one side and then the other side of the selvedge, creating a candy cane stripe effect down your stem. The stripe provides visual interest in your work, a relief from all the solid ribbon.

❋ BIAS TUBING—with or without cording or wire.

❋ VELVET BIAS TUBING—with or without cording or wire.

❋ VARIOUS DECORATIVE CORDS.

❋ SUTACHE BRAID—a trim that's easy to stitch down. It has a channel running down its center.

❋ FLORIST CORD WITH WIRE—in a variety of colors.

❋ PIPE CLEANERS.

❋ STEM WIRE—available in various gauges, covered with green or white thread. Buy the gauge that will support your work, probably #16–#24 gauge, in 18" lengths, on spools and in rolls.

❋ SHINY GREEN EMBROIDERY THREAD—wrapped around stem wire or narrow cord.

❋ CHENILLE—wrapped around cord or wire.

❋ NARROW RIBBON (⅛"–¼")—wrapped in a spiral down your cord or stem wire. Spiral with narrow variegated ribbons to create a candy stripe.

❋ GREEN STEM WIRE AND A NARROW RIBBON twisted together. My introduction to this technique was a ¼" pink satin ribbon twisted with green wire to create a candy-striped stem.

❋ TWO PIECES OF NARROW RICKRACK—intertwined. This stem is quite flexible.

❋ GREEN CHAIN OR FEATHER STITCHES—embroidered.

Vintage rose with twisted ribbon sepals, open berry bud calyx, and pipe-cleaner stem. c. 1950s. Made by Fern Feingut.

It's not a street sign and it's not a lollipop.
It's a leaf on a stem or a flower on a stalk.
It sways and arches, bends and dangles,
weaves and waves and winds and tangles,
but best of all, it dances.

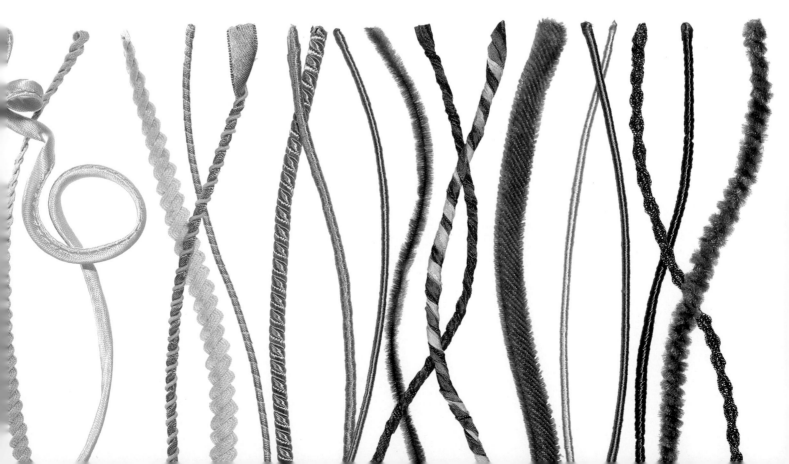

TEXTURED FINISHES

Ribbons are woven with various textures: satin, velvet, and grosgrain, to name a few. Sometimes they are pleated, ruffled, or wired in the manufacturing process. If you know how to make only one ribbon flower, you could still vary it with a repertoire of textural changes.

You can buy textured ribbons, but you can also create them, especially using wire-edged ribbon. You can texture your ribbon using your hands, various tools (irons, etc.), or by stitching. How you pleat and fold, crimp and crush, coax and cajole, adds interest and variety to your work. Creating texture is part of your own personal handwriting. Texture creates visual interest.

For many texturing processes it's hard to calculate how much ribbon to use. I don't cut my ribbon. I just stretch it from time to time as I texture it, until it seems to be enough. Then I cut. You'll create different textural effects depending on whether you add your texture before or after you stitch your flowers and leaves.

Milliners' Shot-of-Steam

Your hot, moist breath and a firm hand will help form soft folds in your ribbon. As you bring the ribbon to your mouth, breathe on it, crushing the folds tightly with your fingers.

Opposite page: Cloche hat with boldly pleated ribbon flowers. c. 1918-1922. Collection of The Oakland Museum of California, History Department. Textiles courtesy of Ana Lisa Hedstrom.

Ruffled Edges

Some ribbons have built-in ruffled edges, but you can also create your own by applying a small ruffle to the outer edge of your ribbon. Vintage ones like this were often done by hand. Don't be concerned if you can see your stitches. They add to the texture. You can also hand-gather close to the outer edges of your petals, but don't pull so tightly that you hide your stitches. They are another element of your design. Another look can be created by pulling the wire at the outer edge of the ribbon.

RUFFLE BUILT-IN

RUFFLE ADDED

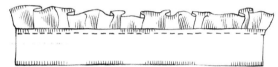

HAND GATHERED

OUTER EDGE

PULLED WIRE

Hand Pleating

Hold the ribbon vertically in front of you. Using both sets of fingers, draw the ribbon toward you, pleat by pleat. First pinch across the top into a fold with your thumbs and index fingers, then push the ribbon up from the back toward you with your middle fingers and press again. Repeat the process, first across the top, then from the back, to create accordion pleats. You are not a machine. Accept and encourage some variation here. You can do this with wired or unwired ribbon. With wire, the ribbon will keep its place immediately. With unwired, you'll need to press the ribbon very tightly with your fingers to create each pleat.

HAND PLEATING

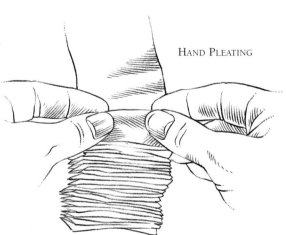

Single-Handed

Pleat only one side of the ribbon. Leave the other side flat. The ribbon will form an arc as you are doing this. Use the same motion as for hand pleating, this time using only one hand. The pleating might be the spine of the leaf, or its outer edge.

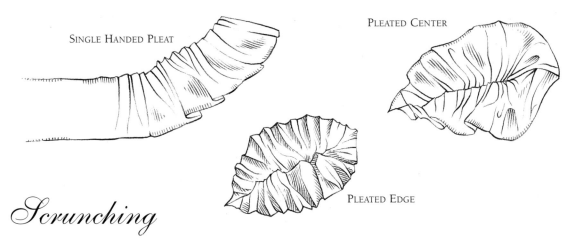

SINGLE HANDED PLEAT

PLEATED CENTER

PLEATED EDGE

Scrunching

Scrunching is not pleating. Feed the ribbon pleats (wired or unwired) into your opposite hand in a random way, with little ⅛" folds. I call this helter skelter, because the pleats are not regular. They're going "every which way." Leave no fold unfolded. Wad up the little pleats into your fingers and thumb. Hold them there tightly, in a little ball, with enough pressure to change the color of your fingertips. You are trying to scar the ribbon.

You can steam or wet your ribbon at the beginning of this process to achieve a more intense texture. Put an elastic band around the wadded up ribbon until it is dry. Ribbons with a polyester content relax a bit after being pleated or scrunched. They don't retain the memory of their distress as strongly as some other fibers.

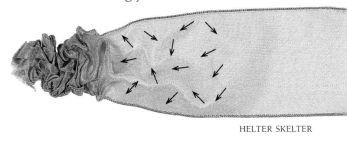

HELTER SKELTER

When applying scrunched ribbon to your ribbonwork composition, loosen your ribbon wad as much or as little as desired, but do notice that it has shrunk to about half its width in the scrunching process, and plan accordingly. Along with its many overall uses, this technique, in a solid green ribbon, makes excellent background foliage. It has the ability to be molded and shaped. See "Scrunchy Leaves" (page 90).

Embracing Old Age

To create the look of fatigue you might find in a ribbon that has been in a trunk for a hundred years, crumple the ribbon as described in scrunching. Then iron those wrinkles flat, but don't steam them out. This will give the feeling of permanence to the worn look, as the ribbon will appear crisp, but not entirely void of wrinkles. It will never be new again.

The Wet Look

Place your wet ribbon (wired or unwired) on an ironing board. Walk your fingers, both hands together, along the ribbon, pinching it in as you go. A loose or firm hand will create different degrees of pleat. The ruffled edges created with this technique can be very random. You might walk the ribbon in a zigzag motion, three steps to the right, then three steps to the left, for a sawtooth effect on the edge. Pin the ribbon to a padded board (page 106) to secure, if necessary, while drying. For a stiff ruffle, try wetting with pump hair spray instead of water.

Vintage flower with petal edges stiched to form gathers. Collection of Carole Sidlow of Romantic Notions.

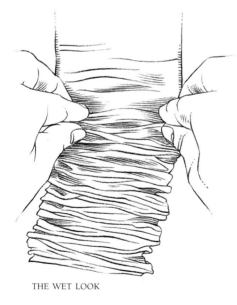

THE WET LOOK

Sit on It

Flattened flowers are useful in the practical sense of wear and washing, but they can also add dimension to your work by providing contrast to your ruffles.

You might take your finished flower (wired only) and press it between the pages of a book. It may not stay flat after this process. You may need to tack it to crinoline. See "Flatbuds" (page 38). A different look is created if you use a shot-of-steam to flatten your work. Use your iron to press down on your ribbonwork, hovering ¼" above the ironing board. Give your rose/ribbonwork a shot-of-steam. Lift the iron and flatten your ribbon with your hand or in a book until dry. If you are reluctant to do this to the first flower that you make, make two instead and squash one of them.

Sign in, Please

Take a hold of the ribbon. How boldly or delicately you treat it, with fingertips or wholehanded, changes the look of your ribbonwork. It personalizes it. It is your signature on the ribbon.

Know When to Quit

You need to create a dialogue between textures. In one area the ribbon scrolls, in another it pleats. It wrinkles and scrunches and crinkles and crumples. The eye gets bored when it finds the same texture throughout your work and it gives up exploring. The eye stays entertained when different parts of your work contain different textures. They speak to each other.

Picking and Poking

You'll need a tool to help you coax the ribbon into place—to work the wired edges, to pick and poke and lift and scroll, especially in tiny areas where your fingers won't fit. I've used a tapestry needle, knitting needle, chopstick, toothpick, or skewer, as well as an African porcupine quill, for this purpose. Depending on the job, you'll need a rounded and a pointed instrument: rounded to form your ribbon without catching in it; pointed to lift it. I pin my ribbonwork first to crinoline and then to a padded surface, then I have both hands free to "sculpt" my ribbon.

Ruffle-edged ribbon flower spray. c. 1920s Collection of Jules and Kaethe Kliot of Lacis.

Not a Halo

The scrunched and pleated, crinkled and rumpled ruffle around your bud is not a Christmas tree skirt lying flat on the floor. It is a dancing girl kicking up her heels. Don't forget to give the ribbon some spirited movement.

A pair of contemporary interpretations of the ruffle-edged flower spray opposite. Created by Zenaida Cosca.

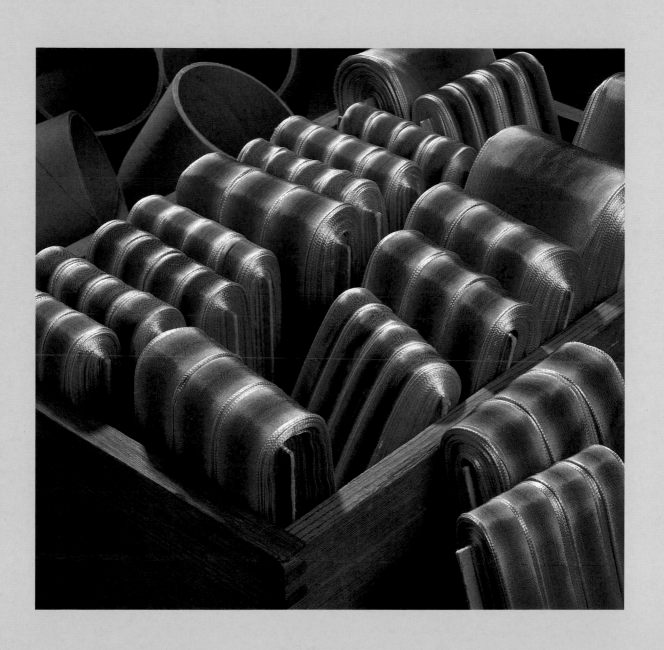

GETTING

What is RW?

RW is your ribbon width. All the ribbon formulas in this book are measured in Ribbon Widths (RW). For example, 5 RW is the width of your ribbon times 5. This single formula works for any width of ribbon and takes the math out of the method.

To measure your ribbon, first establish your ribbon width on a surface with pins or marks. To do this, place your ribbon vertically on your work surface. Put a pin (or mark) on each side of the selvedge as shown. This distance is your Ribbon Width (RW).

Turn the ribbon so it is horizontal and move it along the pins or marks, counting out your formula in Ribbon Widths along the selvedge edge.

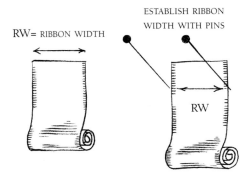

RW= RIBBON WIDTH

ESTABLISH RIBBON WIDTH WITH PINS

RW

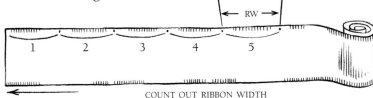

RW

1 2 3 4 5

COUNT OUT RIBBON WIDTH

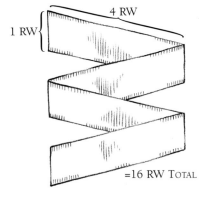

4 RW

1 RW

=16 RW TOTAL

Sometimes you can count by folding your ribbon. For example, to measure a 16 RW length, count four RW and fold to get multiples: 4, 8, 12, 16 as shown. Try 2, 4, 6, 8 or 5, 10, 15, 20. This method is especially useful when measuring longer lengths of ribbon. These folds can also become the markings of the divisions for the Multi-Petal Flowers (pages 45–51).

Opposite page: Bolts of vintage French rayon (rayonne) ribbon. c. 1930s. Collection Ruban et Fleur.

Collecting Ribbon

It's necessary to have a collection of ribbon. All the components of a bouquet take time to accumulate. You need an artist's palette of ribbons, but also bits of floss, cording, lace, beads, stamens, and special buttons. You may not use it all in a lifetime, but you need it to make choices and for inspiration.

Buying Ribbon

Ribbon is available in a profusion of colors, textures, weights, widths, and fibers (cotton, rayon-acetate, silk, and polyester). All of these characteristics will affect the outcome—so experiment. Buy three yards of several different flower colors to get started—you'll be able to make several flowers. Two yards of green should make a handful of leaves. Choose solids as well as ombre/variegated. You'll probably have leftovers. Your collection has begun! As you develop an interest in making ribbon flowers, you may want to buy your ribbon by the roll. It's cheaper that way. You'll always have enough to make extra petals and buds for your compositions, it offers you the freedom to play without having to calculate amounts or costs. If you see a ribbon you like, but you're not sure what you might do with it, buy at least three yards. For help in choosing colors, see "Color" (page 130).

Caveat Emptor

"Caveat emptor." Let the buyer beware.

A word of caution about collecting vintage ribbon: Buy them if you will, covet them if you must, but the vintage ribbons, still on their rolls with paper between the layers, may have deteriorated. Although you would think the paper would have protected them, the reverse is true. This layer of tan paper used to be white, and its acids are eating the ribbon.

To test vintage ribbon, tug hard against the grain, ⅛" from the raw edge and the selvedge, to see if it breaks. I may still buy it because of its beauty, but I'll know not to put it under the stress of stitching.

Care and Feeding

Spend the time to roll the shorter cuts of wire-edged ribbon you are buying while you're still at the store. The employees wrap the ribbon around their hand in a roll. By the time you get home, the rolls get flattened and the wires get crimped. I roll the ribbon myself. I give the beginning of the ribbon three or four ¼" folds and then I roll the remainder of the ribbon around this core. Take your ribbon off its paper backing if you know you're not going to use it soon. Secure the roll at the selvedge (not the middle), pinning through only two layers. (No tape allowed. It leaves a residue.) Store the ribbon away from light and dust. I use artists' flat file drawers for my smaller rolls of ribbon, as well as for beads, buttons, stamens, and leaves. Large single-layer boxes or drawers will give you easier access for decision making.

As beautiful as the ribbons are when they're all rolled and neat, sometimes you need to bring them out and toss them like a salad, just to see how they mix.

Ironing Ribbon

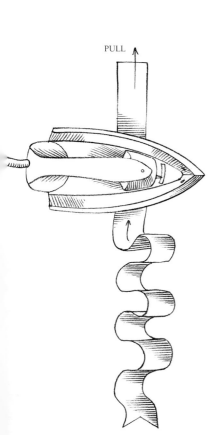

Place the iron on top of your ribbon so one raw edge peeks out. Pull the entire length of ribbon through with one hand, keeping pressure on the iron with the other. Just because it's ribbon doesn't make it delicate. The setting of your iron should match the fiber content of your ribbon.

Wash Day

The flatter your ribbonwork is, the smaller its elements are, and the more you've tacked it down, the better it will survive machine washing. For example, the flower on your bra weathers this process because it is so small.

It is sometimes possible to soak your ribbonwork in water, using a product for fine hand washables. Use a flat pan or sink bottom, gently pushing up and down to clean. Rinse and let dry on towels. To send your ribbonwork to the drycleaner, tack netting over it first to protect it.

The exposed wire on the edge of the ribbon is all that now holds together this "shattered" and sometimes transparent bouquet. c. 1920s. Collection of Arlene Baker.

Bringing Old Girls Back to Life

Use a shot-of-steam iron and a curling iron to revitalize squished, squashed, and crumpled petals, and especially bow loops. Cotton balls and Q-tips are also useful for puffing out the flattened forms while you give them a shot-of-steam. Sometimes wetting the ribbon will work to ease out old crease lines, but you do take a chance, so test one element first.

Padded Surface

Pinning your ribbonwork to a padded surface frees both of your hands to sculpt the ribbon. This freedom also aids in composing. Make a padded board by covering a piece of wood with half-inch thick industrial felt (available at tailors' supply stores). Cover it with cotton twill pulled tautly and use a staple gun to secure the raw edges on the back of the board.

Weather Report

Don't leave your ruffles or drawn-up (but not secured) gathers in place overnight if you plan to continue to work or rearrange the ribbon. Even minimal moisture in the air will act as a shot-of-steam, leaving the ribbon with memory lines and wrinkles that you may find difficult to alter later. Leave the elements of your work in progress flat until you are ready to continue.

Hair Spray

Historically, lacquer was used to stiffen ribbon flowers. Today, you can use pump hair spray for much the same effect. Use hair spray to stabilize and to sculpt. It will be slightly sticky to the hand. Your ribbonwork will need to be held in place until dry. The spray hardens and stiffens without being totally rigid. It dries to a sheen or a shine, but it is not permanent and therefore not washable. If resprayed, the ribbon can be reworked. Test first to assure the desired effect.

Picture This

Ribbonwork can be photocopied. The copy machine seems to love textiles. Whether color or black and white, it records every delicate stitch. The flatter the ribbonwork is, the more successful it will be. The results make pretty stationery and are often better than a snapshot for communicating detail.

Ribbonwork and its photocopy equivalent resting on a 1920s lace sleeping bonnet. Collection of Jennifer Osner.

Leaving Your Mark

I mark my ribbon with a Carb Othello chalk-type pencil, available in fine art stores. It is very soft and chalky. It has no wax or oil in it; no bond that will leave a stain. You can't sharpen it with a pencil sharpener. You have to use a blade. Sometimes it dusts off before you finish your stitching. As far as I'm concerned, that's exactly what I want, something that will disappear. I use yellow, white, or pink. If I know the marks won't show after construction, I may use a standard #2 lead pencil, but with caution, since I wouldn't want the lead to transfer.

Thread

For most ribbonwork, use a thread like cotton-covered polyester that isn't slick. With nylon or silk thread, your gathers will slip and slide rather than staying where you put them. Where possible I use Coats Dual Duty Plus® Buttons, Carpets & Crafts, Topstitching & Buttonhole Twist, or Hand Quilting threads. Heavier thread gives you confidence. It's stronger. It feels more comfortable against your hand when you tug it and it doesn't cut into your skin. You'll work faster as a result of it. However, heavier thread doesn't come in as many colors. You will do most of your tacking in the folds of the ribbon, so your thread is in the shadow. By the time you gather the ribbon down tightly, you don't see the thread color. The color of a pink ribbon in the shadow often appears gray; it's neutral. If a matching thread is not available, it's a dressmaker's or tailor's secret to use a neutral color of thread. This works well in ribbonwork also. You'll need a range of gray, taupe, and khaki colors. For tacking where it may show, choose whatever thread type is pleasing to your eye. Consider these stitches as another design element to your work. If you can't hide them, embrace them.

Don't use the old thread on those beautiful wooden spools that you found at a garage sale or in your grandmother's sewing basket. Textiles have a life span. Old thread slows you down. When you tug on it, it can break. It makes you timid. Use new thread to ensure your ribbon bouquets will live on into the future. Let these old threads decorate your sewing room.

Needles

Alas, you can't have a favorite needle. When I'm in the throes of production, I have an arsenal of threaded needles ready to go. So do some of my students when they come to class. A longer needle is necessary because a good deal of your time in ribbonwork is spent doing running stitches and loading up your needle with gathers. You'll finish the work more efficiently. There is one thing in those old sewing kits you might seek out—the long, strong, narrow needles with the long, gold eyes that will take your heavy thread and still stitch delicately. The closest I've come in a modern needle is a #10 milliners.

Pins = Nails

Don't hammer pins into the outer edges of your ribbon flowers! Depending on the fiber of your ribbon, the holes may not correct themselves very well. Pins have the potential to damage your ribbon. Whenever possible, pin in the folds, "in the ditch," or "in the valleys." The head and point of your pin can flatten your ruffles, pin from the back instead of the front, if you can. Working from the back, catch a minimal amount of ribbon, preferably in the valley fold. Don't leave pins in overnight in an area that will show. The moisture in the air acts like a shot-of-steam and makes the pin marks and distortions permanent. Dressmaker, florist, and hat pins are all useful in ribbonwork.

Vintage pins in their containers. Collection of Arlene Baker.

Duck Clips

Duck clips (3" aluminum hair clips) act as the extra fingers in your ribbonwork.

Use them to hold together fans and sprays of leaves, petals, and loops as you contemplate their positions in your composition. Use them to hold ruffles, petals, or buds to crinoline before you stitch. One clip can hold five leaves, whereas you'd need at least four to five pins to do the same job. Pins can distort as well as damage the ribbon.

Duck clips are available in beauty supply stores in 2" and 3" lengths. A mini-version of these is a ¾" alligator clip used in electrical work and available at hardware stores.

Beginning to Stitch

To begin a row of stitches, thread your needle and knot the end. Pull the needle through the ribbon. Backstitch around your knot. If your knot is on the selvedge, backstitch over the selvedge. Tug the thread to test whether it's secure. A ribbon with a very open weave may require backstitching a second time. Secure your knot to begin stitching.

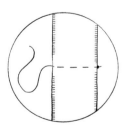

You'll be more comfortable doing your ribbonwork if you try to remember to move the ribbon, instead of the needle or your hands, as you work. If your wrists "hook" as you hold the ribbon, you may need to adjust (and reverse) the position of your ribbon in order to relax them.

Stitch Lengths

How big do I make my stitches? Start with your most comfortable stitch length, the one that seems to come naturally. It's more relaxing work if you can pull this off, because it's more automatic. Still, it's important to have a repertoire. Some effects cannot be created without ⅛", ¼", or ½" stitches.

These rules may apply. The wider the ribbon, the bigger the stitch. The thicker the ribbon, the bigger the stitch. With velvet, for instance, you might start with ¼" stitches. To decide on a stitch length, dive in! Do one (petal, leaf, etc.). If it doesn't work, change your stitch length and do another. In the time it takes you to puzzle over which stitch length might be right, you could have made three and compared them.

Quilters' Challenge

Quilters pride themselves on their tiny stitches. In ribbonwork there are times when you won't be successful in creating an effect unless you make ½" or longer stitches. The most puzzling effect in ribbonwork is that the smaller your stitches, the less the ribbon will condense and the larger the stitches, the tighter it will condense.

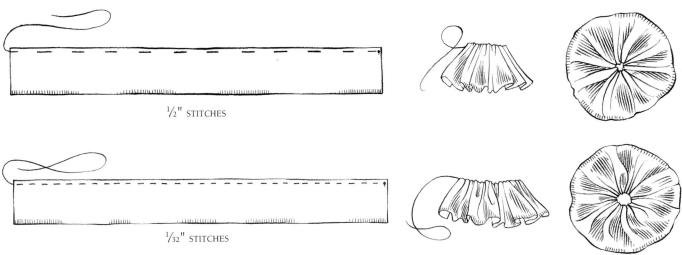

½" STITCHES

1⁄32" STITCHES

This becomes crucial when trying to make small centers for your flowers. Big stitches make little centers, little stitches make bigger centers.

Designed for Comfort

If the execution of that tiny hole is too great a challenge, you can eliminate the issue by designing a flower who's center will be covered with a bud or button. I call this designing for comfort.

Random Running

Ribbon flower work is not like other needle arts, where you are judged on precision. A "too regular" stitch may create a "too regular" set of petals, not at all as nature would intend. All of your stitches need not be the same size. If they are uneven, it will make your little mountains and valleys different sizes. I call this random running.

Gathering

To begin a row of stitches that will be gathered, knot your threaded needle, then pull it through the ribbon. Backstitch around your knot. If your knot is on the selvedge, backstitch over the selvedge. Tug the thread to test whether it's secure. Secure your knot to begin stitching. When you've finished stitching and begin drawing up your gathers to create tiny flower centers, don't be afraid to tug them. You're using heavy thread and you've secured your knot. Go back over the gathers several times with your fingertips, walking along the row, systematically condensing it, little by little, from beginning to end. If you've hand stitched next to a wire, you may need to go back over your row of gathers two or three times to condense it. Sometimes removing the wire where you're going to gather is a good idea. Wire next to gathering can protrude through the selvedge, as little loops, and be unsightly. The wire also adds bulk. Without it you will create a more delicate finish.

Circular Stitching

When doing circular stitching (for a berry bud or daffodil cup), don't begin with a knot at the seam. Choose another spot at random. This feels odd at first, but you'll see its logic as you glide past the seam with your gathering stitches, and later you are able to draw in their bulk more easily, having avoided 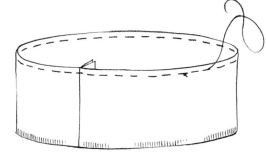 the convergence of two seams with two knots. When ending a row of circular gathering stitches, don't stop short! Your last stitch should overtake your first one; then, when you draw down your stitches, there won't be any (unsewn) gap. This will help you create nice tight centers for your buds or flowers.

Knotting under Tension

To knot without having your gathers loosen in the process, hold the gathers tightly with the thumb and index finger of one hand. Hold your needle with the other. The thread should hang loose in between. Backstitch through your last stitch, then knot. The backstitch secures the end for a moment, so you can let go to make your knot.

Make the Knots Kiss

Use this technique when drawing together petals, or a ruffle, into a circle. First, finish your last petal, backstitch, and knot, but don't cut your thread. Direct your needle back through your beginning knot. Tug tight, closing the gap to "make the knots kiss." Hold the gap together, backstitch, knot again, and then cut your thread.

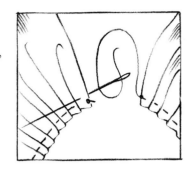

Wire-Edged Ribbon

Available for use in ribbonwork is a ribbon with tiny wires woven into its selvedge edges. The built-in wire makes it easy to sculpt the ribbon. Wire-edged ribbon is so responsive, you can coax it into a myriad of shapes. Basically, though, wire-edged ribbon is for "still life." Imagine you've made a perfectly fabulous corsage, with wire-edged ribbon, which you've secured at the waist of your party dress. You bend to touch your toes. You straighten up, but the ribbon doesn't. If you wore that same corsage at the shoulder, you'd never be able to put your coat on. If a wire-edged ribbon flower were on your hat, though, there would not be a problem.

Not My Good Scissors!

Protect your good scissors from the wire. Have a separate pair for cutting wire-edged ribbon.

Introducing the Wire

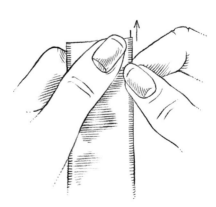

To find the wire, first clean cut the end of your ribbon. Hold the ribbon with the thumb and index finger of one hand, and hold the selvedge with the thumb and middle finger of the other. Push on the selvedge. The wire should peek out the end. (It may be as little as ⅛".)

Using your free index finger, flatten the wire at a 90° angle. This will prevent it from retreating back into the ribbon. Even if you can't see it, you can feel to do this.

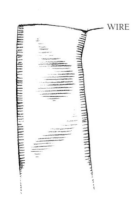

WIRE

Gathering on the Wire

Using the wire to gather, instead of stitches, is a very common process in ribbonwork. There are numerous ways to accomplish gathering on the wire, but this is the most efficient. Pull out 1½" of wire and crimp it backwards on itself. Secure this end of your ribbon by pinning it to a padded surface. From the opposite end, pull out enough wire to be able to wrap the wire around your closed scissor blades (not your finger, ouch!). The wire will be easier to gather if you are standing back until your ribbon is taut. Get up from the table if you have to. Start at the end with the wire-wrapped scissors. The ribbon won't be bouncy or jumpy because it's taut. The ribbon will ease down the secured wire. Holding the wire-wrapped scissors in your dominant hand, push the ribbon down the wire until it logjams (as little as 1"). Don't force it beyond this point. Repeat this process by taking a new handful of ribbon and pushing it down the wire away from your scissors until it logjams. As you move the ruffle forward, you will create a gap. You'll need to fill this gap in small motions. Every time you move a new bit of ruffle forward, your hand moves backward toward your scissors, loading up your ruffles against it to fill the gaps created. With every motion of your hand you're taking a full load of ruffles. There is an economy of movement.

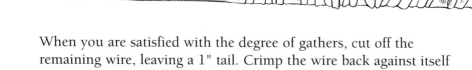

When you are satisfied with the degree of gathers, cut off the remaining wire, leaving a 1" tail. Crimp the wire back against itself to hold the gathers.

Discard the wire. It is not useful for most ribbonwork, except to make tendrils or decorative curly centers. The used wire can have little kinks in it that make it susceptible to breaking.

Going to Extremes

Some ribbons gather very quickly and easily. Others gather more slowly, because the channel the wire goes through seems to stick and the weave of the ribbon doesn't condense as much. These are not reasons to avoid such ribbons. They're just reasons not to commit to making fifty roses out of a particular ribbon you've never tried, for a given amount of money, by Saturday night.

Wiring Your Own

You can wire your own ribbon by taking its selvedge edge and pressing it to form a casing which you then machine sew. Just because the wire is so tiny, though, the casing doesn't have to be. The casing could be huge. It doesn't matter that the wire is floating in it. But don't waste the casing with its selvedge edge by turning it to the back. Instead, fold the selvedge to the front, introducing it as another element of the design, perhaps a fancy stripe for your flower edge.

Often you will only want wire on one edge of the ribbon. Consider your design and plan accordingly. Even bows may need wire on one side only to create a lively gesture.

When you wire your own ribbon or fabric, use a gauge of wire that supports its weight. The smaller the gauge number of wire, the heavier the material that it will support. Most current wire-edged ribbon contains #16 and #25 gauge wire. To wire your own ribbon, use #26–#34 gauge beading or florist wire to support most ribbon and fabric weights.

This process will be easier if you are making separate small wired pieces. After stitching your casing you could pre-cut all of your elements. This way you would only have little pieces of wire to push through instead of three yards of continuous casing. Take ¼" of the end of the wire and make a slightly rounded bend in it as if you were making the eye of a needle, so it will glide through the casing effortlessly.

You can also add wire with your serger. The cording foot has a hole to introduce wire, cord, or fishing line into the stitches.

"But I Paid for that Wire!"

Certain techniques require the removal of the wire. Wire removal is necessary when trying to achieve tiny centers for your flowers. Hand stitching next to the wire can prove bulky when you draw in your gathers. Sometimes loops of wire can pop out of the selvedge and look unsightly. You may take the wire out because your object will be handled and the ribbon needs to bounce back. It's not a "still life." Often I'm purchasing the ribbon more for its color than for the wire anyway.

To remove a wire totally (especially from a longer length of ribbon), secure one end of your ribbon to a padded surface as in "Gathering on the Wire," (page 112). Introduce your wire at the opposite end, wrapping it around your closed scissor blades. Move a handful of gathers along the entire length of ribbon to open up the wire channel. Sometimes this is easy; other times the wire is very snug in the weave and fights this process. Keep working the ruffles down the taut wire until the wire is released. Pull to remove the wire.

Looped Wire Imperfections

Sometimes the ribbon has looped wire imperfections showing through the selvedges. If you notice them ahead of time, you can often design or cut around them, but sometimes they make an unexpected appearance right in the middle of your finished flower. Just clipping them off is not an option, as you can never get close enough without trimming off some ribbon in the process. Stick a pin through the loop and pull it out of the ribbon ¼" or so, clip the wire close to the edge of your ribbon, then pull on your selvedges to draw the wires back inside.

Eek! The Wire Broke!

Stop right where you are! Don't pull the rest of the wire out and don't loosen the part of the ribbon that is already gathered on the wire. You can usually recover a broken wire through the selvedge. First, search for the end of the

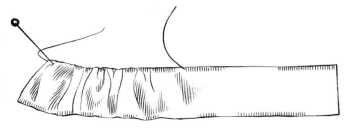

wire. The ribbon will be limp without it. Roll the ribbon at this point and you may see the wire peek out like a needle. Grab it and continue your process.

The thinner gauges of wire act like needles. They will pierce through the selvedges. The heavier gauges won't do this, because the weave of the ribbon is too dense. In this instance, crimp the wire near the broken tip between your fingers. Your pinched loop will be strong enough for you to be able to push it through the edge of the ribbon.

Sometimes you pull out a broken wire completely. Other times it breaks in the middle of the ribbon, leaving a gap. If this happens you'll have to recover the wire in two directions. You may have to hand gather a small empty section, but it's better than having to hand stitch the entire length of ribbon.

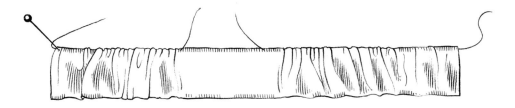

Frayed Selvedge

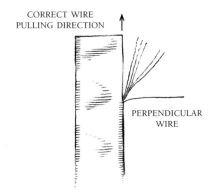

CORRECT WIRE
PULLING DIRECTION

PERPENDICULAR
WIRE

Sometimes as you pull the wire the selvedge will start to fray. If this happens, notice the position of your wire. It's probably perpendicular to the selvedge edge of your ribbon. Avoid further fraying by always pulling the wire parallel to the selvedge. This will be easier if you have secured the other end of the ribbon with a pin.

This fraying only happens on one side and in one direction on some ribbons, so test first if it's crucial. If the ribbon frays, pull the wire from the opposite end instead. More often than not though, the frayed edge can be tucked and hidden in the process of tacking your finished flower or leaf to crinoline.

CRINOLINE

Crinoline has been used for several hundred years as a backing for many flowers and trims. It looks like cheescloth. Do the bulk of your ribbonwork on crinoline. This will allow your garment to remain free of these stitches. Then tack your trimmed crinoline pieces, with a minimum of stitches, to your garment (wedding gown, pillow, baby booties, curtain heading, tablecloth edging, or Civil War replica gown). It is not necessary to fill the train of your silk charmeuse wedding gown with thousands of stitches that would shrink and distort such a beautiful flowing textile. Your flower sprays on crinoline become accessories. Use them to revamp an old garment, embellish a new one, or give a single dress or hat more than one look. The same piece may be worn at the waist of one dress and the neckline of another. Crinoline allows for easy removal to change looks or to launder. You'll learn to love it. You can work on a soft silk backing instead, but then you have to put it in a frame or embroidery hoop.

Opposite page: If it doesn't show, it doesn't count. Every gesture is caught (and caught again) by stitching to the crinoline in these vintage roses. Collection of Jules and Kaethe Kliot of Lacis.

Left: Crinoline back of vintage spray. c. 1920s. Collection of Sandy Fisher. (Front on page 6).

Different Weights

Crinoline comes in different weights and is sometimes called light-weight buckram. If you use wider or heavier ribbon or fabric, you may need medium- or heavy-weight buckram to support it. The stiffened crinoline and buckram act as mock embroidery hoops, stabilizing your work.

Black or White

Crinoline is available in black and in white. Although you are using it as a backing, it may be visible between the elements of your ribbonwork. If seeing it is an issue, you can place fabric the color of your ribbonwork on top of your crinoline before you begin to form your ribbon on it. Try using black crinoline as a backing. It disappears in the shadows of your ribbonwork. As your ribbonwork evolves, you will use more black than white.

Flat Buds, Finally

There are great freedoms in using crinoline. The ribbon isn't stitched to itself as much as it is stitched down to a backing. If you haven't known about crinoline, you may have ended up with a thick glommy mass behind your ribbon flower—a conglomeration of stem, petals, and leaves all converging in a mass of stitches in a single spot at the center back. Eek! Also, there were certain flowers you couldn't make, flat buds especially, because there was nothing to stitch to.

With crinoline all the little parts and pieces, center buds, petals, ruffles, stems, and leaves, are made separately and then layered. You build the flower and whole sprays of flowers with multiple layers of crinoline. Because most of the pieces in ribbon flower work are made separately and individually, you can be working at putting them together, pinning and repinning, until you get them just the way you want them. It's not like beading or embroidery where once you've done it, it's fixed. With crinoline, making all the separate pieces, you retain a degree of flexibility of placement. A large spray of flowers may be made in several sections which, when applied, allow the garment to remain fluid. These same pieces can be arranged and rearranged to accommodate themselves to different garment shapes, decorating a V-neckline one week, or lining a hatband the next.

Itsy Bitsy Teeny Weeny

Even seed beads and French knots can be stitched onto crinoline. Look closely and you will see crinoline peeking out the sides of many of the flowers pictured in this book. If you look closely at the fronts of many of the flowers and leaves, you will notice tiny stitches throughout the work. The flowers are so seductive, they are so beautiful, and

Above and right: Vintage pink rosebuds nestled against ruffles of green ribbon, mass produced on crinoline in France for export. c. 1920s.

Opposite page, top: Flower spray on crinoline still carries its manufacturer's label.

Opposite page, bottom: Six separate petals, individually pleated at the base and gathered at the edge, comprise each of these vintage flowers. They were stitched one by one to the crinoline, which was then trimmed away close to the ribbon edges. Even the stems are wrapped with ribbon. c. 1920s.

All photos: Collection of Jules and Kaethe Kliot of Lacis.

we get so emotionally involved with them, we don't notice little edges of crinoline peeking through or tiny stitches holding the ribbon in place.

Tacking to Crinoline

Cut your crinoline slightly larger than the approximate size of your finished piece. Round the edges where possible.

When tacking to crinoline, place your thumb over the area of the ribbon you want to pin or stitch. Find the pad of your thumb with your pin/needle from the back of the crinoline and come through to the front. Stitch your ribbonwork to crinoline as you would with an embroidery hoop, up from the bottom, down from the top. The tacking on the back of the crinoline can be very random, and very messy, as you decide to put one more stitch here and one more stitch there, drawing your thread back and forth across the crinoline as you go. It takes many stitches on the back to create the impression you want on the front. In ribbonwork, if it doesn't show, it doesn't count.

119

HIDDEN STITCHES

Tack ruffles in the direction of their folds with ⅛" stitches hidden in their valleys. On many flowers this will look like rays of the sun. This secures their gesture and allows you to tame errant folds, drawing them back down to the crinoline.

If you must tack the outside edges of a flower or leaf, make tiny stitches that wrap over the selvedge, perpendicular to the edge of the ribbon. If your thread is thin, and its color matches, you'll be able to draw it down into the ridges of the selvedge. It will disappear. If the outside edge is on a fold, attach the flower to crinoline with a small running stitch hidden in the folds.

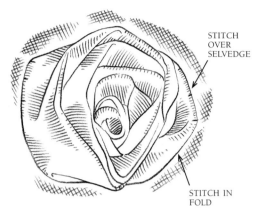

STITCH OVER SELVEDGE

STITCH IN FOLD

Layering Crinoline

More complex flower work is done by layering your crinoline. You might form your bud and stitch it onto crinoline. Trim away excess crinoline around the bud edge as close to your stitches as possible. Make leaves, ruffles, and/or petals and tack them down securely to another crinoline piece, instead of trying to tack them under the bud. Stitching everything to one piece of crinoline is awkward and not very secure, and might result in stitches showing on the front of the bud. Tack the pre-made bud on top of the petal/leaf composition. Clip away all excess crinoline on the back. Leave only enough to hold the gesture. Tack as many times as makes you feel secure. Even the leaf gesture is done on the crinoline. Nothing is left to chance, or to gravity, or to the reckless touch of an admirer.

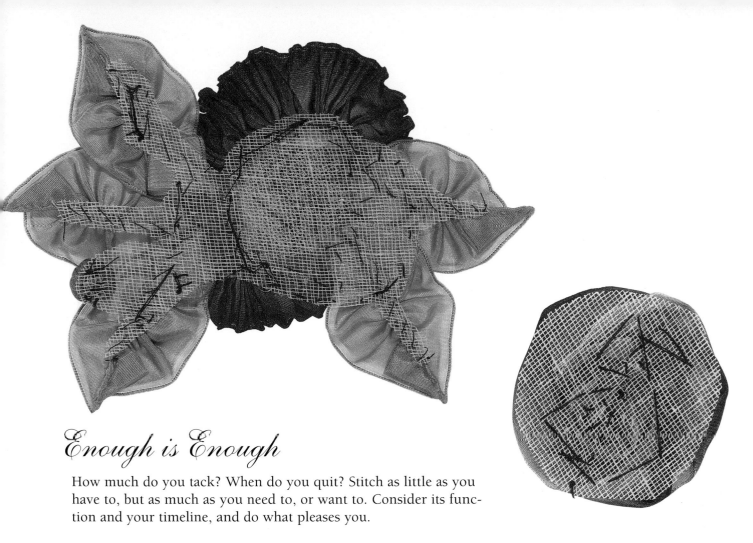

Enough is Enough

How much do you tack? When do you quit? Stitch as little as you have to, but as much as you need to, or want to. Consider its function and your timeline, and do what pleases you.

121

THE DANCE

Flowers in a Vase

We all have a relationship with flowers. It may be slightly different than that of women in the past; we may not paint china or draw roses on our valentines, but many of us still grow flowers, and arrange them in vases. It is this process of arranging that so closely resembles that of creating ribbon flower bouquets. Unlike embroidering and beading, most of the elements of this work are made separately and independently. It is not until the very end of the process, after arranging and rearranging your ribbon flowers, that you tack them down. This allows you enormous freedom of composition.

The Opera

I like to think of ribbon flower compositions as mini operas. They have principal players and a chorus, colorful costumes, dynamic staging and lighting, choreographed movement, and a rich palette of color. The best ribbonwork uses all these elements to create a rich drama.

The Tenor and the Soprano

Every opera has its principal players. More time, effort, and expense goes into making their costumes. These costumes have pearls tucked into their folds and beads trimming their ruffled edges. Just what you should do to your more dominant ribbon flowers. These main flowers are usually larger than others in the composition and may be of a single flower type. Still, you might vary their color. In your garden, where you planted the mixed packet of sweet peas and roses the colors range from blush pink to deepest scarlet, the form is the same, but the colors vary.

The Chorus

Previous pages: Dresden ballerinas typify the grace and the beauty that is the "dance." Collection of Candace Kling.

The opera also has its chorus. If you went backstage and looked at their costumes, you'd be disappointed. They're not elaborate, but they fill the stage. It's not their complexity but their sheer numbers that impress us. They make the stage feel rich. Apply this idea to your ribbon bouquets. You need lots of filler flowers to tuck into the gaps and spaces in your flower arrangements. They shouldn't distract from the main attraction. They aren't as showy and impressive as the principals, but they make your whole bouquet look rich.

In ribbonwork these are often smaller flowers of entirely different varieties from the main ones in your bouquet. Some might take a few minutes to make and a few inches of ribbon gathered to form a circle. But you make dozens of them. You go into production, becoming a little flower making machine. You might also mix some purchased trims and buds into your bouquets. They can add bulk and fullness at a minimal price with only the effort of shopping.

You may not need a totally finished drawing of this work, designating the position of each flower exactly. You will know the shape you want to fill: a hatband, the toe of a wedding slipper, the tieback of your Victorian curtains. You make your principal players and place them, then fill in with your chorus.

Not a Coloring Book

The drawings for your work, if you choose to have them, are not like those in a coloring book, or like traced embroidery where you fill in between the lines. You can be more flexible here. Each finished flower is different, so you have leeway in arranging them; nestling them closer together or spreading them apart as need be, tucking in extra leaves, petals, and buds as you see fit. You mustn't be too rigid in sticking to your original composition. Let the flowers have their way!

From Buds to Full Bloom

In many ribbon compositions, especially the more complex ones, you will notice that not all the flowers are in the same state of maturity. Some are budding while others have burst into full bloom. If you've ever tried to get all the flowers in the garden to bloom on the wedding day, you already know that it will never happen! Flowers don't all burst into bloom simultaneously. If you are trying to create a sense of naturalism, group together flowers in various stages of development.

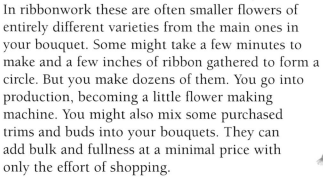

Above and below: Collection of Jules and Kaethe Kliot of Lacis.

Left: Vintage postcard. Collection of Meron Reinger.

Getting Perspective

As you place flowers, one by one into a vase, some will look up, others down, some toward you and some away. This creates what is called perspective. It creates depth and a feeling of three dimensions. You can achieve this in your ribbon flower work by changing the positions of the flower centers, the eyes of your flowers. You don't want your flower work to look like a class photograph, with all eyes looking at you. Flowers are not targets, and you are not a cookie press. Don't stamp them out all looking the same.

There are several easy ways to give ribbon flowers gesture. Sometimes it's as simple as not making the center sit up and stare at you. Take the coiled center and lay it on its side to create a three-quarter view, eyes to the side. Or you might place your petals or ruffles on only one side of your budded center. The petals of your flower are not like the rays of the sun in a child's drawing. Even sunflowers, which follow the sun, have slight movement and gesture.

Modesty Shows Her Face

Flowers in three-quarter view or flowers in profile, are art terms to describe forms of perspective. These gestures also create flower personality. Flowers in profile have "bonnets" covering their faces, although sometimes they peek from behind their petals. Flowers that look down or away are described as having a modest or shy gaze. By contrast, sunflowers gaze straight at you with eager smiling faces.

All the World's a Stage

Another type of perspective is created in the theater, on stage. The city of Verona is painted on a hung backdrop; while the actors are swordfighting, down front in the footlights. In your flower work you mix flat elements with dimensional ones to achieve this sense of depth through contrast. Work an embroidered, painted, or printed background with dimensional petals or leaves, or make the budded centers of your flowers very flat and surround them with extremely dimensional ruffled petals that cloak the bud.

Baby's Breath and Queen Anne's Lace

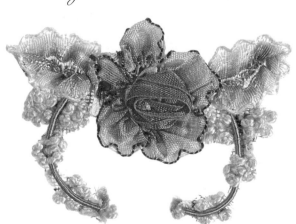

French knots and seed beads are the baby's breath and Queen Anne's lace of your bouquet. They add a delicacy and an airiness to your work. Stamens can also contribute to this lacy quality. They can all help create a change of scale by contrasting in size to your larger ribbon flowers.

Above: Collection of Jules and Kaethe Kliot of Lacis.

Opposite page: These blush-pink floral forms were individually made by hand and mounted onto crinoline for export from France. Note that they are very similar but not exactly alike. c. 1920s. Collection of Sandy Fisher.

Left: Crinoline secures the tiniest French knots in this vintage flower cluster. c. 1920s. Collection of Jules and Kaethe Kliot of Lacis.

Let's Talk About the Weather

Go outside early in the morning and you might see dew drops in your garden. They sparkle. They catch your eye as you walk by. They make you know the world is alive. In your ribbon flower work include metallic ribbon or lace, glitter on your stamens, little seed beads or rhinestones to make it shimmer. This is not a blizzard of rhinestones, just an accent. As you walk past it, or it walks past you, it's going to catch your eye. It's going to wave at you.

Grazing at the Checkout Stand

As you are waiting in the grocery line, look at the home and garden magazines. You can learn things about how nature mixes color from the photos of flowers in them. In spring you might turn the pages and see shocking pink tulips with apple-green stems mixed with lavender-blue delphinium. Or turn to the summer issue and find sunflower yellow enhanced by a deep, rich, rusty brown (center). You'll notice lots of blue flowers. Make them a staple of your ribbonwork. Delphinium, larkspur, forget-me-not, lobelia, and iris, are all magnificent mixed with the yellows and pinks of spring.

You may also come to realize more strongly your own taste in color. You'll go beyond the "favorite color" concept. At first glance you might respond positively to a bouquet of pink roses. But look again and realize they aren't all pink. They're actually pink and white with chrome yellow centers!

Color

Most flowers have a natural iridescence. That's why they don't clash. Most colors will work together, depending on how much of each you use, and what accent colors you include in the mix. It's not a question of which colors match or clash. Again, let nature be your teacher. If you discover a vase of red and pink roses pleases you more than one mixed with yellow, white, and coral, this color preference may cross over into your ribbonwork. When you go to the ribbon rack it seems natural that you would buy certain colors because they're your favorites. In flower work, you "embellish" your favorite colors. What makes colors sing are the accents you put with them. You may not be attracted to acid green and chrome yellow, but that little touch of chartreuse or bright orange gives life to your deep violet. Black and white add elegance to your mix, but on the rack can be neglected. Alone, white seems flat and plain, but it won't when you work in black stamens or a fluffy, glowing, golden center. Flat black sings with the addition of white, chrome, and red. Stamens, seed beads, and French knots can become your accents of color.

This is where all those little bits and pieces you've saved will come in handy; adding a needed accent of a slightly different color. Snippets as little as two or three ribbon widths are enough for a small bud or leaf. Save everything! If you start to study nature a bit, you'll understand the accents and the whole palette of color you need, instead of just buying your "favorite color."

I recommend you buy some colors by the roll. Every artist needs an inventory, an existing palette of colors to play with, even though you will undoubtedly find yourself out shopping for one more pink, two more lavenders, or three more greens. In the long run it will be cheaper, since ribbon is less expensive by the roll. Ribbonwork is very seductive. You won't want to stop after just one rose. If you're going to indulge in any experimentation, you need to stock up. This will give you the freedom to manufacture extra parts and pieces, as well as extra presents!

If It's Green, It's a Leaf

The leaves, stems, and tendrils in your ribbonwork are like the arms and hands of the Russian dancer who is complimented for her fine "finish." They are the fingertips of your dance, giving life and movement to your work. Leaves are living things affected by wind, water, and light. In your ribbon-work they are affected by your stitches and your touch. As you twist and bend them, the viewer's eye is drawn around and through the piece, willingly following arching spines and wayward

tendrils. Like the nineteenth century etchings of bows with their flowing tails, this movement should make your heart sing.

Green is nature's balance in your bouquet. It can excite or subdue your colors. Green is synonymous with life. There's a coolness to it and an element of protection. It's the color of shade. Under the trees you feel sheltered and relaxed. Green is a restful color. Green is nature's home.

In ribbonwork, if it's green, it's a leaf, especially if it's green and pointed. But sometimes green is the setting, the backdrop for your flowers. It's lawn and shrubbery. Ribbon flowers often nestle on a ruffle of green ribbon that looks more like filler foliage than specific leaves. Sometimes it resembles lettuce, or a doily, and gives the flowers a corsage effect.

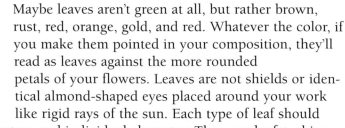

Maybe leaves aren't green at all, but rather brown, rust, red, orange, gold, and red. Whatever the color, if you make them pointed in your composition, they'll read as leaves against the more rounded petals of your flowers. Leaves are not shields or identical almond-shaped eyes placed around your work like rigid rays of the sun. Each type of leaf should have individual gesture and individual character. They can be fat, skinny, round, oval, or ruffly. Make some matte and some shiny. Give them a variety of textural finishes. One large leaf may overpower a single flower, yet be dwarfed among several flowers. Leaf proportion is related to the size of your composition and the number of its elements.

Start looking in those home and garden magazines at bouquets. As you walk by your local florist, take in the color combinations. Get a feel for the percentage of green you respond to. Is the bouquet half green? Or only 10 percent? How many greens are in it? Every leaf and every stem of each type of flower, front and back sides too, all are different greens. Gray green, mint green, apple green, forest green, kelly green, seafoam, olive, celadon, and khaki. Start mixing your greens. You may come to realize what you want to collect more than anything is green (ribbon). It can be hard to find. The exact color you want may not be available. In the garment industry greens have the maddening tendency of changing every season, making it impossible to match last year's sweater with this year's skirt. This is an advantage in ribbonwork. The more greens you collect, the better. Eventually you'll have a whole palette.

The Bride Wore Black

In vintage ribbonwork they often strayed from an all-white palette in both their infant and wedding garments, introducing the palest shades of pink, coral, lavender, lemon yellow, and ice blue for buds, petals, and bow loops, and taupe and mint green for stems and leaves. If you do choose a single color palette, white for bridal, say, or black for cocktail, rely on form to distinguish petals (round) from leaves (pointed).

Above: Ringed with lace and accented with tips of green ribbon, this line-up of vintage rosebuds is as simple as it gets. Collection of Arlene Baker.

Right: It took a bit of everything to construct this corsage. The three green leaves forming an outer triangle help to rein in the diverse elements in this vintage composition. Collection of Carole Sidlow of Romantic Notions.

Opposite page: Budded blooms cluster on an embroidered and lace trimmed batiste dress. c. 1920s. Collection of Arlene Baker.

"Mirror, Mirror..."

Look at your work in a mirror. Many artists do this. It doubles its distance from you, and by reversing the image, depersonalizes it. The mirror will give you a fresh take. You will be more objective in critiquing your work, and more kind in your own praise.

132

As Much as You Have To, As Little as You Can Get Away With

If this work is a hobby, you have the luxury of indulging in all of the loving finishing touches. But if it is applied to objects you sell, you may need to use speed, efficiency, and cost cutting instead. Your personal agenda affects how you approach and finish the work. Tack it down as much as you have to and as little as you can get away with. And remember, in ribbonwork, if it doesn't show, it doesn't count.

Sometimes function plays a part. An object that is going to be handled or laundered needs more stitching to ensure its security. A "still life" (wreath, hat, or picture) needs less. But you may not be happy unless you've tacked it to within an inch of its life! Please yourself. Time also plays its part. You might be needing 300 roses for a wedding next Saturday. Stitching goes out the window and the glue gun marches in.

Perfection, Give it Up!

In your ribbon flower work avoid the chorus line, where each dancing gal mimics her neighbor and precision is the last word. Nature doesn't make all her elements exactly the same, as a machine does, and as many stitchers strive to do. Each petal of a flower has its uniqueness. So learn to trust your eye, and refer less often to your tape measure. Instead of measuring each move, develop your own "handwriting." Give the work your personality. It will become your own handwritten letter. I remember well the mixed compliment I received in the early 1970s for a wedding dress I was embroidering. "It's so perfect! It looks like a machine did it." But I did it! I hadn't yet learned to trust my own hand.

For most stitchers perfection lies in creating identical elements. In nature, and in your flower work, perfection is in mixing slightly unidentical elements to create the perfect balance. So strive for perfection, nature's way.

Impressionism

Ribbonwork is not exactly like nature. It has its own unique and flexible set of rules. Daffodils, for instance, may look better with five petals instead of six, just as a cartoon figure does with four fingers instead of five. The simplicity of it reads better. The question is, are you making a replica or the essence of the rose? The best work interprets nature without having to copy it. This was understood by women in the 1920s and earlier. They chose to create their own personal impressionistic "vision" of flowers, softened and smoothed. But their "impressions" were based on observation. Ribbon flowers are inspired by, but need not mimic, Mother Nature.

That Was Then, This Is Now

The flowers of the 1920s were not copies of Victorian ones. Nor were those of the late nineteenth century lifted exactly from those so popular in the eighteenth century. Each era re-invents history and adds its mark. This is what I hope you will do as you use this book.

Left and opposite page: This vintage bounty in a basket combines ruffled ribbons with petals ranging from sheer silk to rich velvet. c. first quarter 20th century. Collection of Arlene Baker.

Appreciation

I know as I write, this book is all made possible because I teach. Many students championed me, taking their samples from my classes back to other guilds, stores, and schools. They have provided the perfect turn of phrase to describe an action, the perfect nickname for a technique. They have created whole new variations. They have enriched the experience. I wish I could credit all of them for their numerous contributions. I hope they recognize themselves in these pages.

The creation of this book was made possible through the encouragement of everyone at C&T Publishing, who enthusiastically embraced the marriage without a "proposal."

I am most grateful to the many generous collectors who loaned their vintage beauties for the photos in this book. I hope I have credited them correctly.

Over the years, many have shared my passion. I am especially grateful to: Michelle Dalton, with whom I first embarked on the research path; Alison Lara for the delicacy of her hand and spirit; Sandy Erickson of Antiquity Press for her entrepreneurial zeal in republishing The *Art and Craft of Ribbonwork* in 1983 and helping to spread the word; Jules and Kaethe Kliot for creating Lacis, in whose rarefied air you will always find a kindred spirit; Inez Brooks-Myers for being my mentor in all matters relating to "dress"; the Costume Society of America for providing me with my more formal education in costume; Marcy Tilton for creating, and Linda Lee for sustaining, The Sewing Workshop, where all my ribbon classes have incubated; Ruban et Fleur for their generous spirit in business and in friendship; Karen Wyse for creating Bizarre Bazaar, and for inspiring me with her descriptive prose; and Melissa Leventon for her blend of wicked humor and wise words.

Books don't write themselves. Mine was created with a great deal of assistance. I wish to thank Beverly Anderson for "Juliet"; Mary Reed for the laptop named "Sweet Pea"; Katie Power, Susie Lee, and Miki Pryor for assisting the computer virgin; Marilyn Pescola for performing the "Last Writes"; Eliza Meeker for the "poetic words"; my proofreaders, Imogene Kling, Dorothy Aggeler, and Ana Lisa Hedstrom; Sharon Pilcher for her immediate and ongoing enthusiasm; Sally Lanzarotti for embracing with good nature and tenacity, the monstrous task of creating a whole new language; Liz Aneloski for entering the game late and still carrying us to victory; Barb Kuhn for understanding the essence and drawing it out; Jill Berry for breathing color into blank pages; Lynda Albiero for her sage advice about lavender, the color with the "phantom scent"; and Diane Pedersen for "naming the baby."

I am grateful to my mother for her love of beauty and of pleasure, for the precision of her words, and for teaching me perfection, so I could give it up; and to my father for his love of words and the craft of writing, and for the realization that if you're lucky, work is fun.

I wish to thank Tracy Johansing Spittler for the luxury of allowing me to trust; Group Nine, with the understanding that it's for life; Rik Olson for his lyrical line; John Bagley for having the master's eye and the friend's heart; Marshall Crossman for her generosity in the eleventh hour; Zenaida Cosca, who after being invited for a day, stayed for a year, and contributed to almost every aspect of this book; and Alex Bergeron, for providing shelter from the storm.

And finally, I wish to thank the two who have believed in me the longest and strongest: Deborah Kimble for being the champion of so many aspects of my career, and for sharing my love of "frou frou"; and Fred Kling for sharing the path that led to being an artist, and believing that it is a righteous one.

About the Author

Candace Kling's sixteen years of enthusiastic research in antique ribbonwork and fabric embellishment have led her to explore both private and museum costume and textile collections across the country—teaching and lecturing as she goes. Her highly detailed textile sculptures have been exhibited in museums and galleries, nationally and internationally over the past sixteen years and have earned her a featured spot in the documentary video, Wearable Art From California, as well as inclusion in the permanent collection of the American Craft Museum in New York. In 1995, she was honored to have her work included in the "8th International Triennial of Tapestry" in Lodz, Poland. Her work has appeared in numerous publications including: *Victoria*, *Threads*, *Fiberarts*, and the premier issue of *Treasures in Needlework*.

In the early years of her research, Candace gave the term "antique ribbonwork" to the blossoming collection of techniques she was discovering. She credits portraiture and flat pattern drafting studies for training her eye to catch the fine details of the stitched and folded ribbons she was discovering. When she began to teach these techniques in 1983 the most commonly asked question was, "What is it?" A dozen years later, the question has been answered—artful ribbon in all of its forms. The world is filled with ribbon enthusiasts, using these techniques to embellish an endless array of creations. With this, her first book, she shares her knowledge, passion, and pleasure for the subject of ribbon flowers.

Ribbon & Trim Sources

ARLENE BAKER
7470 Lubec Street
Downey, CA 90240
310-928-3583
Collector and dealer of vintage ribbonwork.

BELL 'OCCHIO
8 Brady St.
San Francisco, CA 94103
415-864-4048 FAX 415-864-2626
Retail, mail order. Vintage and modern ribbon. Specializing in wider ribbons. Unusual woven ribbons, exceptional vintage metallic ribbons, vintage velvet ribbons and straw ribbons. New millinery flowers, primarily French silk. This store is a beauty, don't miss it!

BRIMAR INC.
1500 Old Deerfield Road, Suite 5
Highland Park, IL 60035
847-272-9585 FAX 847-831-3531
Wholesale, retail, mail order. $150 1st order. Catalog available. Tassels, braids, cording, ribbons, metallics, and more. Special commissions. Tassel workshops.

BRITEX
146 Geary St.
San Francisco, CA 94108
415-392-2910 FAX 415-392-3906
A San Francisco institution; the reverent travel from all parts of the west to shop here. Four floors of fabrics and notions. They're bound to have what you're looking for. Wonderful 4th floor notions, especially the buttons, ribbons, laces and trims. Mostly modern ribbon, but some choice vintage also. Crinoline available.

CLASSIC TRIMS
1925 63rd St. E.
Inver Grove Heights, MN 55077
612-552-9637
Wholesale, retail, mail order, catalog available. Specializes in metallic trims & laces. Line of woven braids (jacquards). Lots of miniature.

ELSIE'S EXQUISIQUES
208 State St.
P.O. Box 260
St. Joseph, MI 49085
616-982-0449 FAX 616-982-0963
800-742-SILK
Wholesale, retail, mail order. Catalog available. Specializes in miniatures for doll makers. Ribbons, trims, miniature flowers, double ended stamens, some vintage ribbon. Also manufacturer of some trims and flowers.

A FINE ROMANCE
2912 Hennepin Ave. South
Minneapolis, MN 55408
612-822-4144 FAX 612-822-9773
Retail, limited mail order. Ribbons, vintage and contemporary ribbonwork. Beautiful store. Lovely ribbon selection. Stamens and crinoline.

FRENCH ACCENTS, INC.
20705 Southwestern Avenue #108
Torrance, CA 90501
310-212-3374 FAX 310-212-3092
Wholesale. $200 first order. Importers of French wired ribbon. Call for Rep. or retail outlet in your area.

GARDNER'S RIBBON & LACE
2235 E. Division
Arlington, TX 76011
817-640-1436
Wholesale, retail, vintage and modern, buttons, ribbons, trims and laces, wire edged ribbon, grosgrain (solid, stripes and polka dots). Rep. for Hymen & Hendler and Elsie's Exquisites. 3 button lines, IJN, Blue Moon & Buttons Etc.

HANAH SILK (Wholesale only)
5155 Myrtle Ave.
Eureka, CA 95503
707-442-0886 FAX 707-442-8453
Artemis (Wholesale and retail)
A Distributor of Hanah Silk
179 High Street
South Portland, Maine 04106
207-741-2509 FAX 207-741-2497
100% silk bias-cut hand-dyed ribbons, Sample cards—$15.00.

HYMEN & HENDLER
67 W. 38th St.
NYC, NY 10018
212-840-8393/4/5
Wholesale, retail. No mail order. Ribbons galore in every style, color, width and price imaginable. They manufacture ribbons in Europe. They carry basic ribbons like satin and grosgrain, also luxurious ribbons, rare morés, plaids, stripes, ombres, metallics, cut velvets, iridescents, elaborate brocades, and tapestry ribbons. Many imported or antique. Also fancy tassels. An essential stop on any NYC trip!

LACIS
2982 Adeline Ave. (at Ashby)
Berkeley, CA 94703 (next to Ashby Bart)
510-843-7178 FAX 510-843-5018
Wholesale, retail, catalog available. An emporium of laces and lace supplies (vintage and modern) and ever so much more. The retail store is a "must see" if you come to the Bay Area. 30 yrs. in business. Lace, ribbons, buttons, tassels, flower stamens, beads, jewelry, clothing, costume and textile books galore, vintage sewing tools, also vintage replicas. Crinoline available. Distributor of Mokuba and YLI.

HATS BY LEKO
2081 Buffalo St.
Casper, WY 82604
307-473-8881 FAX 307-473-8883
800-817-HATS
Wholesale, retail millinery supplies. $30.00 minimum. Millinery classes. This business boasts of having more different kinds of straws and felts than most people have seen under one roof. Also a wide range of high quality and unique millinery items, trims, flowers, ribbons, stamens, vintage and modern. Stock is always changing. They have crinoline. Nice book selection. Call for catalog.

M & J TRIMMING COMPANY
1008 6th Ave. (near 37th St.)
NYC, NY 10018
212-391-9072
Wholesale, retail, mail order ($30 minimum). Extensive trim selection. Also trims for interiors. Braids, ribbons, lace trim, buckles, buttons, sequined and beaded appliqués, loose beads, paillettes, tassels, antique passementerie, fringes, curtain tiebacks, decorative elastics.

MIDORI, INC.
3524 West Government Way
Seattle, WA 98119
206-282-3595 FAX 206-282-3431
Wholesale ribbon, $100 minimum. Contact them for Rep. or retail source in your area. On-time delivery! Japanese ribbon, organdy, satin and taffetas.

MOKUBA CO., LTD.
4-16-8 Kuramae
Taito-Ku
Tokyo, Japan
03 (3861) 2626 (tele. #)
03 (3886) 6288 (FAX)
U.S. Reps. for Mokuba; Quilters Resource (as listed), Silverman Products & Textiles 212-944-8200; FAX 212-869-8881. You will need their 2 sample books for the stock numbers.

Opposite page: Hand-embroidered ribbon tapes from the saris of the Parsai women of India. c. 1900. Collections of Zenaida Cosca, Brenda Henriques, and Candace Kling.

JANICE NAIBERT
165 Emory Lane
Rockville, MD 20853
301-774-9252 FAX 301-924-1725
Wholesale, retail at doll shows, SASE
for list of other retail sources. Ribbons
and trims, vintage look. Silk buds n
bows, silk pleats, vintage buttons and
French laces.

NANCY'S SEWING BASKET
2221 Queen Anne Ave N.
Seattle, WA 98109
206-282-9112 FAX 206-282-7321
800-443-2964
Retail, limited mail order, classes. Great
fabric store. Handwork supplies. Lots of
ribbon in the ribbon room. Full selection of colors of ¼" rococco ribbon.

OFFRAY RIBBON C.M. OFFRAY &
SON, INC.
(also Lion Ribbon Company,
an Offray affiliate)
Route 24, Box 601
Chester, NJ 07930-0601
908-879-4700 FAX 908-879-8588
Major wholesale ribbon sellers. Available
retail in most fabric stores across the
country. Woven edged ribbon, art, crafts,
gift and floral ribbons. Grosgrains, poly
satins. Some exotics, lamés, sheers,
metallics, wire edged solids and ombres.

PAULETTE C. KNIGHT, INC.
343 Vermont St.
San Francisco, CA 94103
415-626-6184 FAX 415-626-2564
800-642-8900
Wholesale importer, retail in showroom.
Source for French ribbon, wired and
unwired (over 100 styles), pleated,
plain, ombre (variegated), gold edged,
striped, plaid, and metallic. Vintage silk
flowers and leaves. Carries some
Renaissance Ribbons in showroom. $200
minimum 1st order. Call for Rep. or
retail stores in your area.

PIECEMAKERS COUNTRY STORE
1720 Adams Ave.
Costa Mesa, CA 92626
714-641-3112 FAX 714-641-2883
Retail. Ribbon, trims, quilt fabrics,
millinery supplies, crinoline. Over 275
different classes each quarter ranging
from quilts to dolls, tole painting, all
facets of needlework and crafts. Class
schedule/catalog available.

QUILTER'S RESOURCE
P.O. Box 148850
Chicago, IL 60614
312-278-5695 FAX 312-278-1348
800-676-6543
Wholesale to stores only. Call for retail
stores in your area. Catalog available.

French wire ribbon, silk ribbon for
embroidery, Italian and Swiss ribbons,
some trims and laces, some books,
assorted vintage ribbon, crinoline, buttons, antique buttons and charms.
Importer of Elegance Ribbon. Rep.
for Mokuba.

RENAISSANCE RIBBONS
9690 Stackhouse Rd.
P.O. Box 699
Oregon House, CA 95962
916-692-0842 FAX 916-692-0915
Primarily wholesale and importer.
Catalog available. Limited retail through
mail order and internet. French ribbons,
braids and trims (woven, jacquard, silk,
wired, metallic), tassels, laces, metallic
laces, vintage ribbons, upholstery trims,
passementerie, fringes and tassels, gift
wrapping ribbon. Japanese and French
organdy ribbons, French cotton/rayon
grosgrain.

CAMELA NITSCHKE RIBBONRY
119 Louisiana Ave.
Perrysburg, OH 43551
419-872-0073 FAX 419-872-0073
Retail, wholesale, mail order, classes.
Catalog available. Ribbons and ribbonwork objects. Japanese ribbon, French
jacquards from St. Etienne, up to 6",
heavily embroidered. Jacquards, floral
and historical, baroque satins, Society
satins, doubly woven, wire edged ribbons, silk ribbons for embroidery, crinoline, books, kits and videos. Beautiful
store, worth a visit.

ROMANTIC NOTIONS
(formerly The Olde Lace Store)
6125 W. Tropicana "F"
Las Vegas, NV 89103
702-248-1957 FAX 702-248-4288
Antique gift store, featuring handmade
one-of-a-kind ladies accessories, using
antique fabrics, trims, ribbons, and buttons. Large selection of French wired
ribbons, vintage ribbon and trims,
antique buttons, antique table and bed
linens, antique lace accessories,
millinery supplies and hats, stamens,
crinoline.

RUBAN ET FLEUR
8655 Sepulveda Blvd. (in Westchester
Fair Antique Mall, 5 minutes from LAX
Airport)
Westchester, CA 90045
310-641-3466 FAX 310-641-1211
Retail, wholesale. Catalog available. Sells
a variety of French wired ribbon, hats,
charms, flowers and stamens, unusual
trims, vintage hat decorations, vintage
velvet and vintage rayon ribbon, jaquard
ribbon and crinoline. Largest selection
of French wired ribbon in So CA. Low
prices and a pleasure to deal with.

TAIL OF THE YAK
2632 Ashby Ave.
Berkeley, CA 94705
510-841-9891
Retail. Gifts, Georgian and Victorian
jewelry, decorative arts. Ribbon, vintage
and modern, wire edged, organza, velvet, grosgrain, novelty, some silk ribbon.
Metallic cording, mesh ribbon, unusual
buttons, fabric flowers, leaves. This store
is a treasure, don't miss it!

THINGS JAPANESE
9805 NE 116th St.
Kirkland, WA 98034
206-821-2287 FAX 206-823-4907
Mail order. White silk ribbon, 2mm,
3.5mm, 7mm, 32mm. Also silk dyes and
dyeing instructions. Kits for dyeing.
Variety packs of ribbon and ready made
roses. 100 weight silk thread in 9 colors,
can also be dyed.

TINSEL TRADING COMPANY
47 W. 38th St.
NYC, NY 10018
212-730-1030 FAX 212-768-8823
Wholesale, retail, mail order (video catalog available). Antique trims for clothing
and interiors. Including metallic braids,
ribbons, fringes, cords, tassels, medal-
lions, bullion's. Metallic trims from the
1900s. A New York institution.

VV ROULEAUX
201 New King's Road
Parsons Green
London, England SW6
071-371-5929
4000 different ribbons: plain, pleated,
polka dot and picot-edged. Ribbons of
silk, rayon, lace and paper. Striped,
appliqué, and moiré ribbons.

VABAN
2070C Boston Dr.
Atlanta, GA 30337
404-991-1315 FAX 404-996-8017
Wholesale ribbon. European manufac-
tured ribbon including wire-edged.
Int: Vaban Ribbon International
      Post Bus 5001
      Sittard, Netherlands
      NL-6130 PA
      FAX 31-46-452-5264

Y.L.I. CORPORATION
P.O. Box 420-747
San Francisco, CA 94142
FAX 415-255-2329
Wholesale, retail. Catalog available.
Ribbon, thread and yarn. Pure silk
Japanese ribbon
for embroidery. Silk thread and floss.
Books and kits.

Suggested Reading

Anlezark, Mildred. *Hats on Heads, The Art of Creative Millinery.* Kangaroo Press, Kenthurst, NSW, Australia, 1991.

Adamich Laufer. *Tussie Mussies, The Victorian Art of Expressing Yourself in the Language of Flowers.* Workman Publishing, New York, New York, 1993.

Beck, Thomasina. *The Embroiderer's Flowers.* David & Charles Brunel House, Newton Abbot, Devon, England, 1992.

Hair Ornaments of Ribbon. Ondori Publications, Japan, 1991.

Herbort, Diane and Bonnie Benson. *Gardening with Ribbons.* Quilters' Resource Inc., Chicago, Illinois, 1994.

Kingdom, Christine. *Glorious Ribbons.* Chilton Book Company, Radnor, Pennsylvania, 1993.

In Style. The Metropolitan Museum of Art, New York, New York, 1987.

Lewis, Annabel. *The Ultimate Ribbon Book.* Trefalger Square Publishing, London, England, 1995

Link, Nelle Weymouth. *Smocking and Gathering for Fabric Manipulation.* Lacis Publications, Berkeley, California, 1987.

Lyday, Cookie. *Country Ribbon Crafts, Delightful Projects Using Easy Techniques.* Sterling Publishing Co., Inc., New York, New York, 1994.

McKinnon, Gloria. *Anne's Glory Box, Book Four.* Fairfax Press, Rushcutters Bay, Australia, 1994.

Montano, Judith Baker. *The Art of Silk Ribbon Embroidery.* C&T Publishing, Lafayette, California, 1993.

Montano, Judith Baker. *Elegant Stitches.* C&T Publishing, Lafayette, California, 1994.

Ogura, Yukiko. *Ribbon Accessories.* NHK Publications, Japan, 1995.

Old-Fashioned Ribbon Art. Dover Publications, Inc., New York, New York, 1986.

Pace, Kathy. *A Ribbon Bouquet.* Pace Publishing, Coalville, Utah, 1995.

Picken, Mary Brooks. *Old-Fashioned Ribbon Trimmings and Flowers.* Dover Publications, Inc., New York, New York, 1993.

Ribbonology. Antiquity Press, St. Helena, California, 1995.

Sienkiewicz, Elly. *Dimensional Appliqué – Baskets, Blooms & Baltimore Borders.* C&T Publishing, Lafayette, California, 1993.

Takahashi, Emiko. *Ribbon Art Technique.* NHK Publications, Japan, 1991.

The Art and Craft of Ribbonwork, Vol. I & II. Antiquity Press, St. Helena, California, 1983.

White, Palmer. *Haute Couture Embroidery, The Art of Lesage.* Lacis Publications, Berkeley, California, 1994.

Woman's Institute of Domestic Arts & Sciences, Department of Millinery. *Ribbon Trimmings, A Course in Six Parts.* Sloane Publications, Martinez, California, 1992.

Index

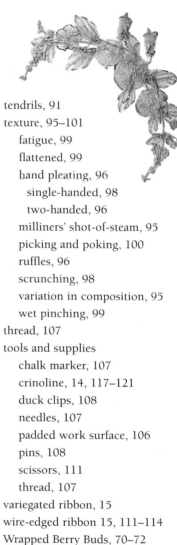

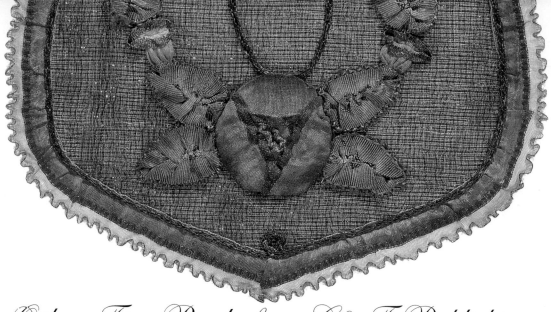

Metallic ruffle-edged ribbon was used to trim the edge as well as construct the buds in this metallic mesh piece. c. 1920s. Collection of Jules and Kaethe Kliot of Lacis.

Other Fine Books from C&T Publishing:

An Amish Adventure - 2nd Edition, Roberta Horton
Appliqué 12 Easy Ways! Elly Sienkiewicz
Art & Inspiration: Ruth B. McDowell,
  Ruth B. McDowell
The Art of Silk Ribbon Embroidery,
  Judith Baker Montano
*Baltimore Album Quilts, Historic Notes and Antique
  Patterns*, Elly Sienkiewicz
Baltimore Beauties and Beyond (2 Volumes),
  Elly Sienkiewicz
Basic Seminole Patchwork, Cheryl Greider Bradkin
Beyond the Horizon, Small Landscape Appliqué,
  Valerie Hearder
Buttonhole Stitch Appliqué, Jean Wells
Christmas Traditions From the Heart,
  Margaret Peters
Christmas Traditions From the Heart, Volume Two,
  Margaret Peters
Colors Changing Hue, Yvonne Porcella
Crazy Quilt Handbook, Judith Montano
Crazy Quilt Odyssey, Judith Montano
Crazy with Cotton, Diana Leone
*Dimensional Appliqué—Baskets, Blooms &
  Baltimore Borders*, Elly Sienkiewicz
*Elegant Stitches: An Illustrated Stitch Guide &
  Source Book of Inspiration*, Judith Baker
  Montano
Everything Flowers, Quilts from the Garden,
  Jean and Valori Wells
The Fabric Makes the Quilt, Roberta Horton
Faces & Places, Images in Appliqué,
  Charlotte Warr Andersen
*Fantastic Figures: Ideas & Techniques Using the New
  Clays*, Susanna Oroyan
Fractured Landscape Quilts, Katie Pasquini
  Masopust
Heirloom Machine Quilting, Harriet Hargrave
Kaleidoscopes & Quilts, Paula Nadelstern
Impressionist Quilts, Gai Perry
Landscapes & Illusions, Joen Wolfrom
The Magical Effects of Color, Joen Wolfrom

Mariner's Compass: An American Quilt Classic,
  Judy Mathieson
Mariner's Compass Quilts, New Directions,
  Judy Mathieson
Mastering Machine Appliqué, Harriet Hargrave
Nancy Crow: Improvisational Quilts, Nancy Crow
The New Sampler Quilt, Diana Leone
*Papercuts and Plenty, Vol. III of Baltimore Beauties
  and Beyond*, Elly Sienkiewicz
Pattern Play, Doreen Speckmann
Pieced Clothing Variations, Yvonne Porcella
Patchwork Quilts Made Easy, Jean Wells
  (co-published with Rodale Press, Inc.)
Quilts for Fabric Lovers, Alex Anderson
Quilts, Quilts, and More Quilts! Diana McClun and
  Laura Nownes
Schoolhouse Appliqué: Reverse Techniques and More,
  Charlotte Patera
Simply Stars, Alex Anderson
*Small Scale Quiltmaking: Precision, Proportion, and
  Detail*, Sally Collins
Soft-Edge Piecing, Jinny Beyer
Stripes in Quilts, Mary Mashuta
Symmetry: A Design System for Quiltmakers,
  Ruth B. McDowell
3 Dimensional Design, Katie Pasquini
*Tradition with a Twist: Variations on Your Favorite
  Quilts*, Blanche Young and Dalene Young Stone
Trapunto by Machine, Hari Walner
A Treasury of Quilt Labels, Susan McKelvey
Visions: QuiltArt, Quilt San Diego
The Visual Dance: Creating Spectacular Quilts,
  Joen Wolfrom
88 Leaders, Nihon Vogue

For more information write or call for a
free catalog from:
    C&T Publishing
    P.O. Box 1456
    Lafayette, CA 94549
    1-800-284-1114